LEHMAN / CRÉTY

MASKED

1 - ANOMALIES

WRITTEN BY
SERGE LEHMAN

PENCILS BY
STÉPHANE CRÉTY

INKS BY
JULIEN HUGONNARD - BERT

COLORS BY
GAÉTAN GEORGES

Titan
COMICS

MASKED

1 - ANOMALIES

WRITTEN BY
SERGE LEHMAN

PENCILS BY
STÉPHANE CRÉTY

INKS BY
JULIEN HUGONNARD - BERT

COLORS BY
GAÉTAN GEORGES

TRANSLATED BY
EDWARD GAUVIN

LETTERING BY
KIRSTEN MURRAY

For my parents. ~ S.L.

Many thanks to Serge, Julien, Gaétan, David, and Guy, our great helmsman.

Many thanks for this adventure in every sense of the word. I dedicate this work to Juliette and Rodrigue, superheroes of my every day, who have so many powers: the power to annoy me with their doe-eyes, the power to trample all over my nerves, the power to ask for more... I love you. ~ S.C.

COLLECTION EDITOR
Nora Goldberg
COLLECTION DESIGNER
Russell Seal
SENIOR EDITOR
Steve White
TITAN COMICS EDITORIAL
Andrew James, Tom Williams
PRODUCTION MANAGER
Obi Onuora
PRODUCTION SUPERVISORS
Jackie Flook, Maria Pearson
PRODUCTION ASSISTANT
Peter James
STUDIO MANAGER
Emma Smith
CIRCULATION MANAGER
Steve Tothill
MARKETING MANAGER
Ricky Claydon
SENIOR MARKETING AND PRESS EXECUTIVE
Owen Johnson
PUBLISHING MANAGER
Darryl Tothill
PUBLISHING DIRECTOR
Chris Teather
OPERATIONS DIRECTOR
Leigh Baulch
EXECUTIVE DIRECTOR
Vivian Cheung
PUBLISHER
Nick Landau

Masked Volume 1: Anomalies
ISBN: 9781782761082

Published by Titan Comics
A division of Titan Publishing Group Ltd.
144 Southwark St.
London
SE1 0UP

A CIP catalogue record for this title is available from the British Library.

First edition: April 2015

10 9 8 7 6 5 4 3 2 1

Printed in China.
Titan Comics. TC0209

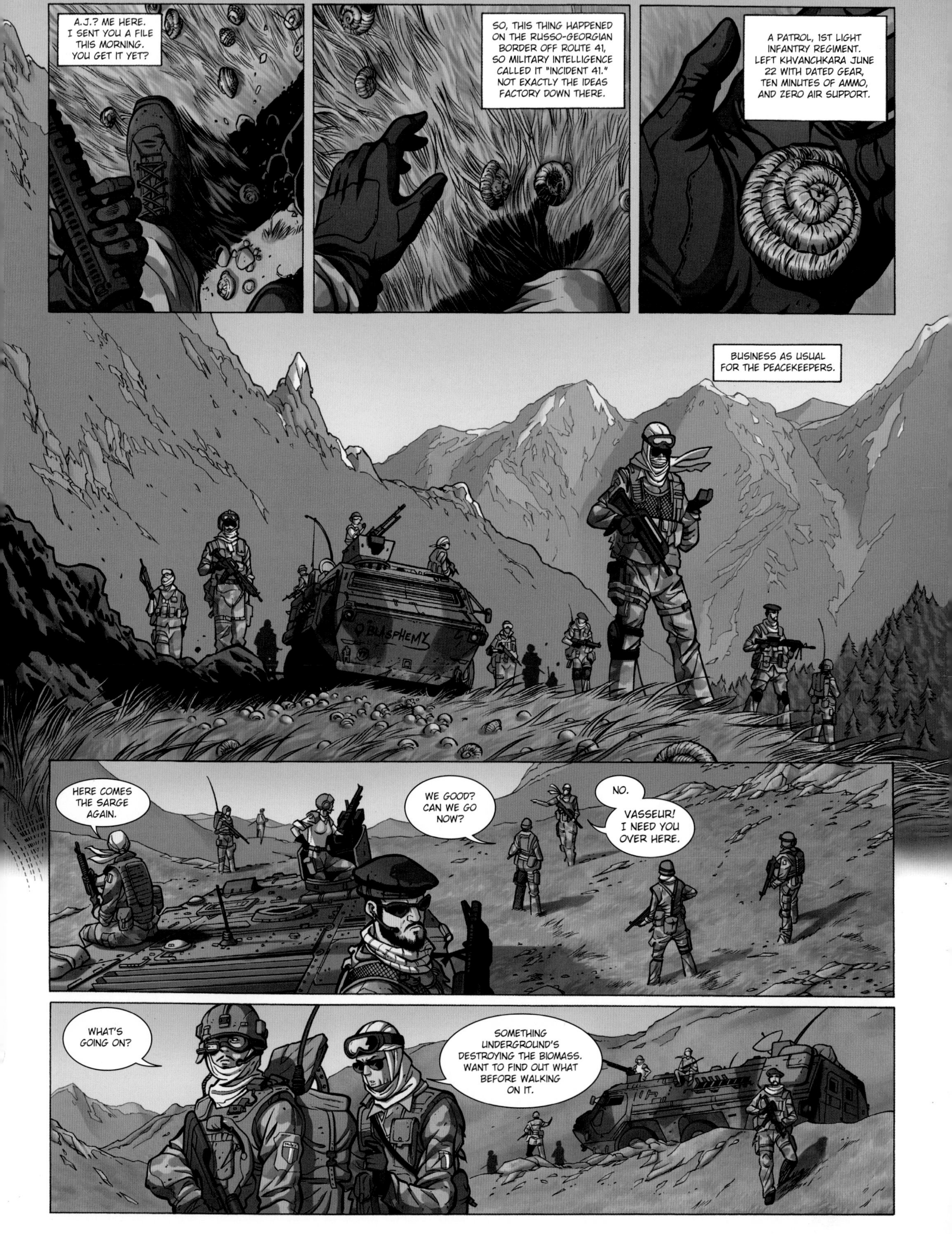
A.J.? ME HERE. I SENT YOU A FILE THIS MORNING. YOU GET IT YET?
SO, THIS THING HAPPENED ON THE RUSSO-GEORGIAN BORDER OFF ROUTE 41, SO MILITARY INTELLIGENCE CALLED IT "INCIDENT 41." NOT EXACTLY THE IDEAS FACTORY DOWN THERE.
A PATROL, 1ST LIGHT INFANTRY REGIMENT. LEFT KHVANCHKARA JUNE 22 WITH DATED GEAR, TEN MINUTES OF AMMO, AND ZERO AIR SUPPORT.
BUSINESS AS USUAL FOR THE PEACEKEEPERS.
BLASPHEMY
HERE COMES THE SARGE AGAIN.
WE GOOD? CAN WE GO NOW?
NO.
VASSEUR! I NEED YOU OVER HERE.
WHAT'S GOING ON?
SOMETHING UNDERGROUND'S DESTROYING THE BIOMASS. WANT TO FIND OUT WHAT BEFORE WALKING ON IT.

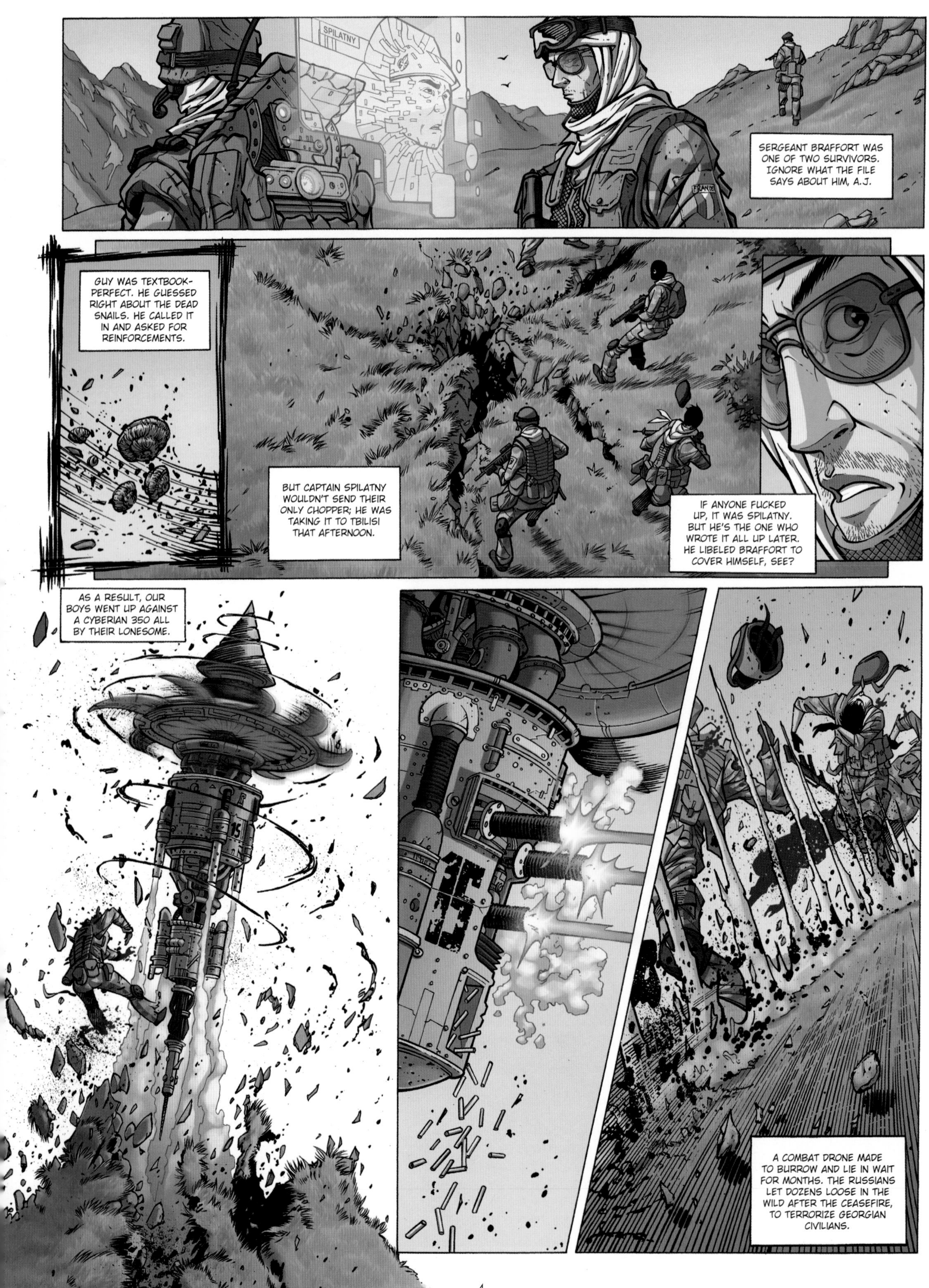
SPILATNY
SERGEANT BRAFFORT WAS ONE OF TWO SURVIVORS. IGNORE WHAT THE FILE SAYS ABOUT HIM, A.J.
GUY WAS TEXTBOOK-PERFECT. HE GUESSED RIGHT ABOUT THE DEAD SNAILS. HE CALLED IT IN AND ASKED FOR REINFORCEMENTS.
BUT CAPTAIN SPILATNY WOULDN'T SEND THEIR ONLY CHOPPER; HE WAS TAKING IT TO TBILISI THAT AFTERNOON.
IF ANYONE FUCKED UP, IT WAS SPILATNY. BUT HE'S THE ONE WHO WROTE IT ALL UP LATER. HE LIBELED BRAFFORT TO COVER HIMSELF, SEE?
AS A RESULT, OUR BOYS WENT UP AGAINST A CYBERIAN 350 ALL BY THEIR LONESOME.
A COMBAT DRONE MADE TO BURROW AND LIE IN WAIT FOR MONTHS. THE RUSSIANS LET DOZENS LOOSE IN THE WILD AFTER THE CEASEFIRE, TO TERRORIZE GEORGIAN CIVILIANS.

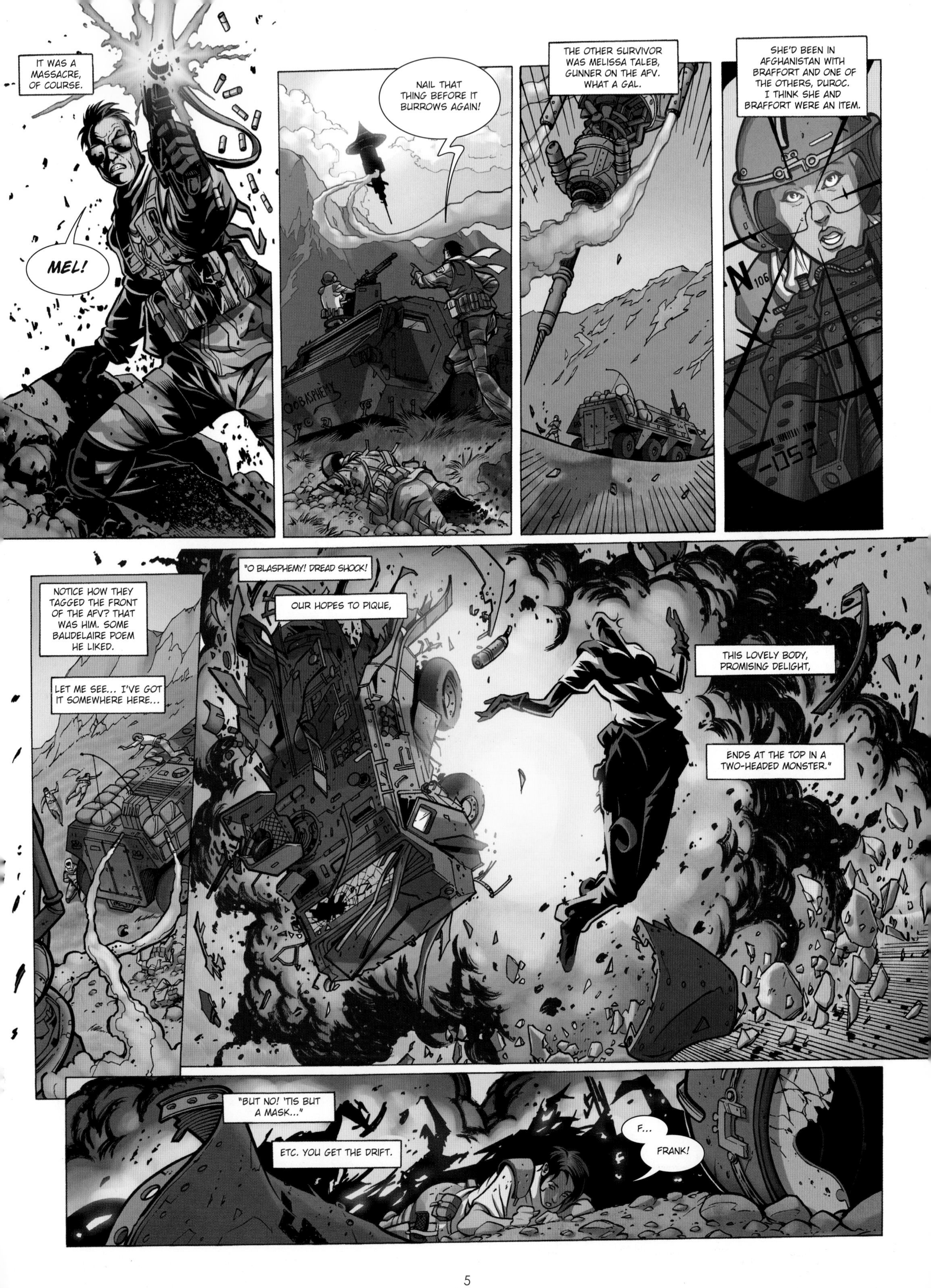
IT WAS A MASSACRE, OF COURSE.
MEL!
NAIL THAT THING BEFORE IT BURROWS AGAIN!
THE OTHER SURVIVOR WAS MELISSA TALEB, GUNNER ON THE AFV. WHAT A GAL.
SHE'D BEEN IN AFGHANISTAN WITH BRAFFORT AND ONE OF THE OTHERS, DUROC. I THINK SHE AND BRAFFORT WERE AN ITEM.
NOTICE HOW THEY TAGGED THE FRONT OF THE AFV? THAT WAS HIM. SOME BAUDELAIRE POEM HE LIKED.
LET ME SEE... I'VE GOT IT SOMEWHERE HERE...
"O BLASPHEMY! DREAD SHOCK!
OUR HOPES TO PIQUE,
THIS LOVELY BODY, PROMISING DELIGHT,
ENDS AT THE TOP IN A TWO-HEADED MONSTER."
"BUT NO! 'TIS BUT A MASK..."
ETC. YOU GET THE DRIFT.
F...
FRANK!

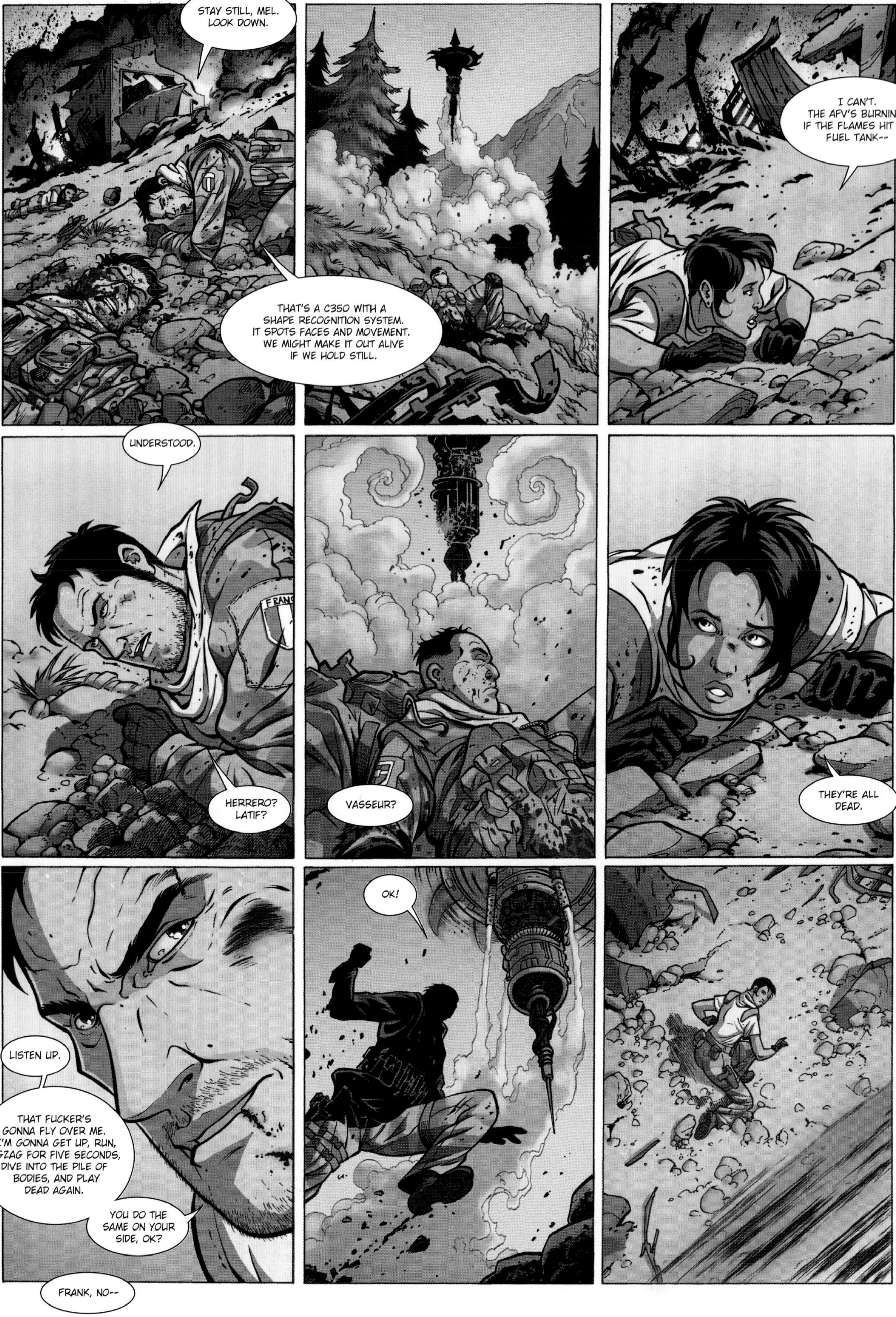
STAY STILL, MEL. LOOK DOWN.
THAT'S A C350 WITH A SHAPE RECOGNITION SYSTEM. IT SPOTS FACES AND MOVEMENT. WE MIGHT MAKE IT OUT ALIVE IF WE HOLD STILL.
I CAN'T. THE AFV'S BURNING. IF THE FLAMES HIT THE FUEL TANK--
UNDERSTOOD.
HERRERO? LATIF?
VASSEUR?
THEY'RE ALL DEAD.
LISTEN UP.
THAT FUCKER'S GONNA FLY OVER ME. I'M GONNA GET UP, RUN, ZIGZAG FOR FIVE SECONDS, DIVE INTO THE PILE OF BODIES, AND PLAY DEAD AGAIN.
YOU DO THE SAME ON YOUR SIDE, OK?
FRANK, NO--
OK!

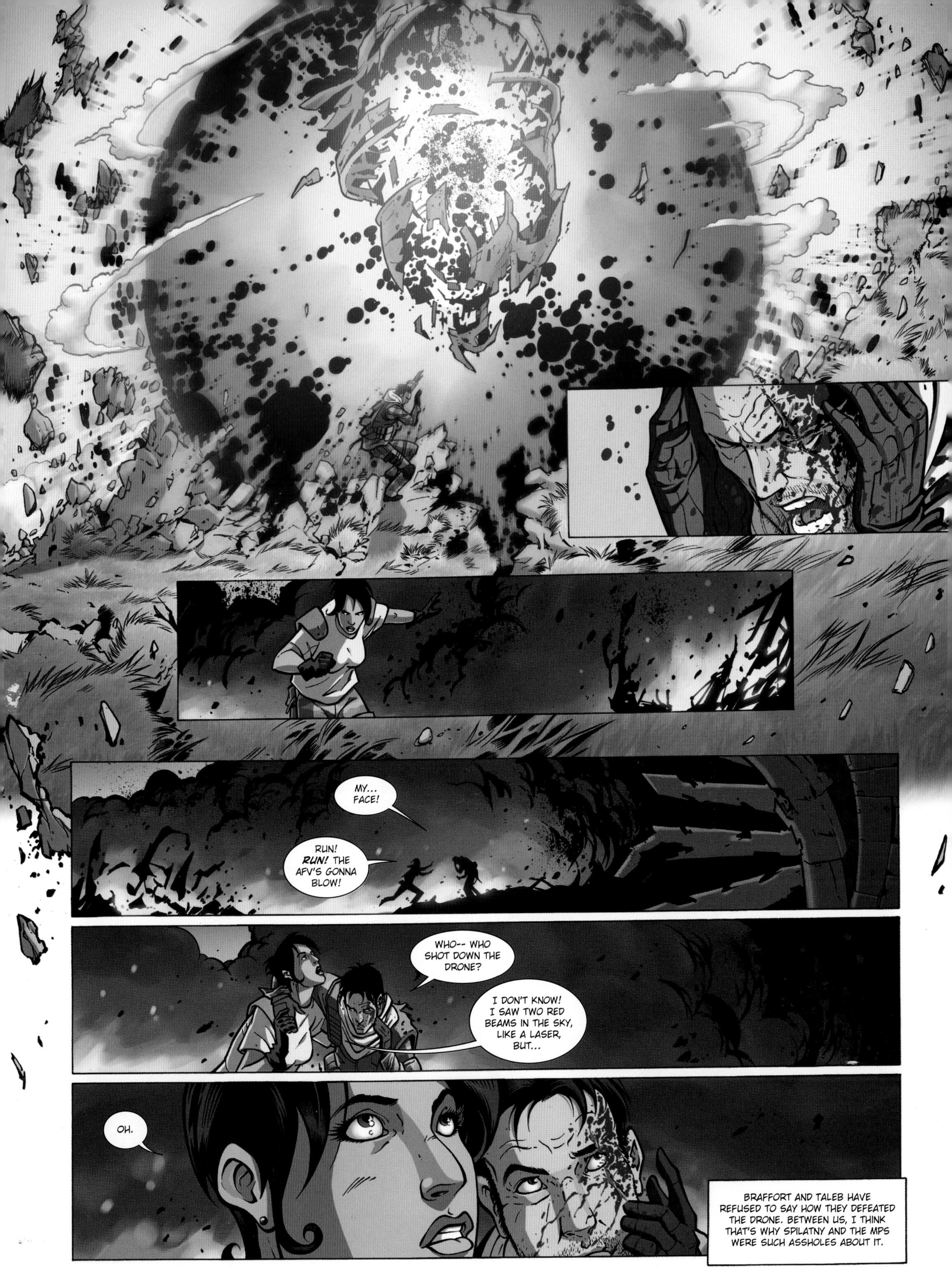
MY... FACE!
RUN! *RUN!* THE AFV'S GONNA BLOW!
WHO-- WHO SHOT DOWN THE DRONE?
I DON'T KNOW! I SAW TWO RED BEAMS IN THE SKY, LIKE A LASER, BUT...
OH.
BRAFFORT AND TALEB HAVE REFUSED TO SAY HOW THEY DEFEATED THE DRONE. BETWEEN US, I THINK THAT'S WHY SPILATNY AND THE MPS WERE SUCH ASSHOLES ABOUT IT.

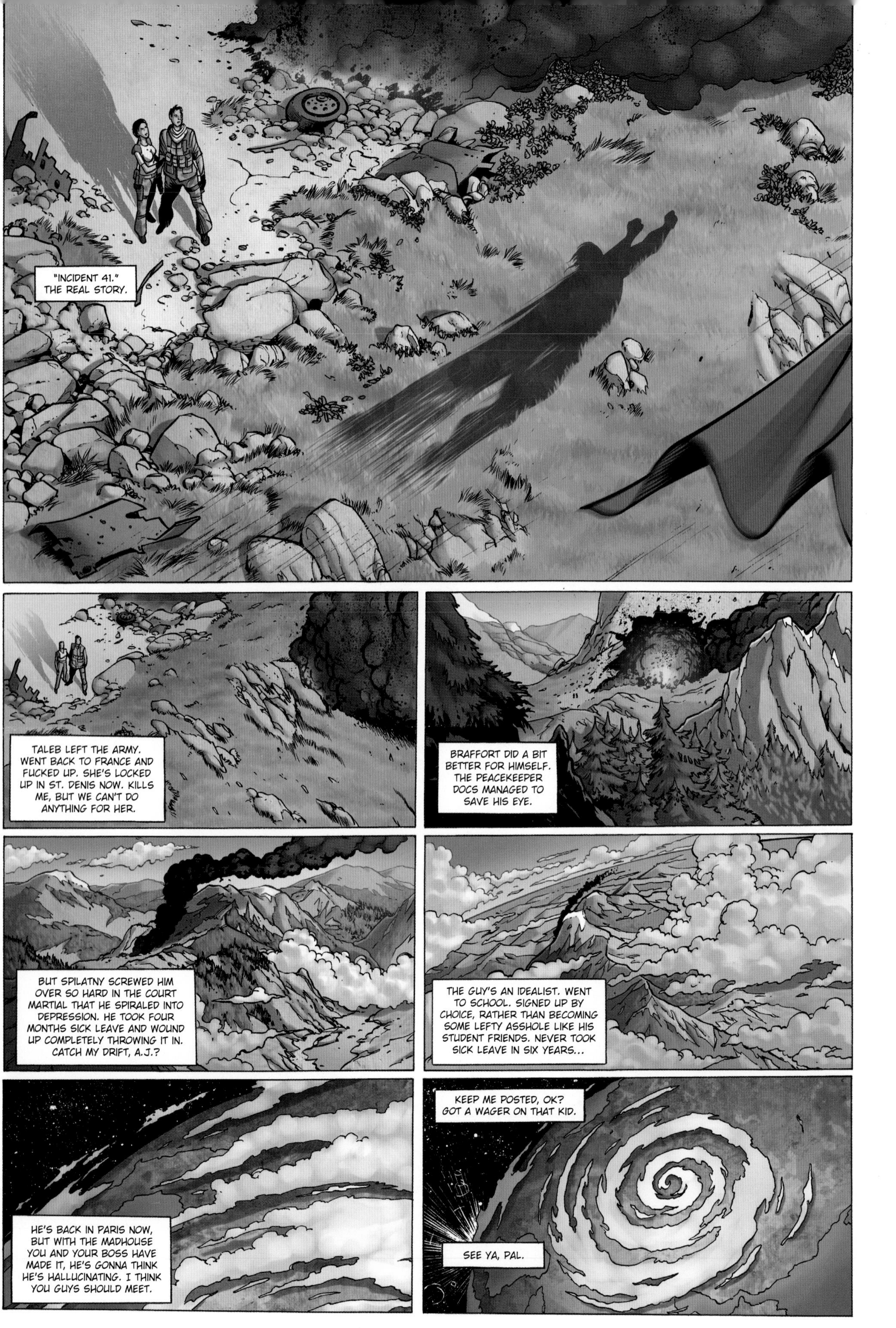
"INCIDENT 41."
THE REAL STORY.
TALEB LEFT THE ARMY. WENT BACK TO FRANCE AND FUCKED UP. SHE'S LOCKED UP IN ST. DENIS NOW. KILLS ME, BUT WE CAN'T DO ANYTHING FOR HER.
BRAFFORT DID A BIT BETTER FOR HIMSELF. THE PEACEKEEPER DOCS MANAGED TO SAVE HIS EYE.
BUT SPILATNY SCREWED HIM OVER SO HARD IN THE COURT MARTIAL THAT HE SPIRALED INTO DEPRESSION. HE TOOK FOUR MONTHS SICK LEAVE AND WOUND UP COMPLETELY THROWING IT IN. CATCH MY DRIFT, A.J.?
THE GUY'S AN IDEALIST. WENT TO SCHOOL. SIGNED UP BY CHOICE, RATHER THAN BECOMING SOME LEFTY ASSHOLE LIKE HIS STUDENT FRIENDS. NEVER TOOK SICK LEAVE IN SIX YEARS...
HE'S BACK IN PARIS NOW, BUT WITH THE MADHOUSE YOU AND YOUR BOSS HAVE MADE IT, HE'S GONNA THINK HE'S HALLUCINATING. I THINK YOU GUYS SHOULD MEET.
KEEP ME POSTED, OK? GOT A WAGER ON THAT KID.
SEE YA, PAL.

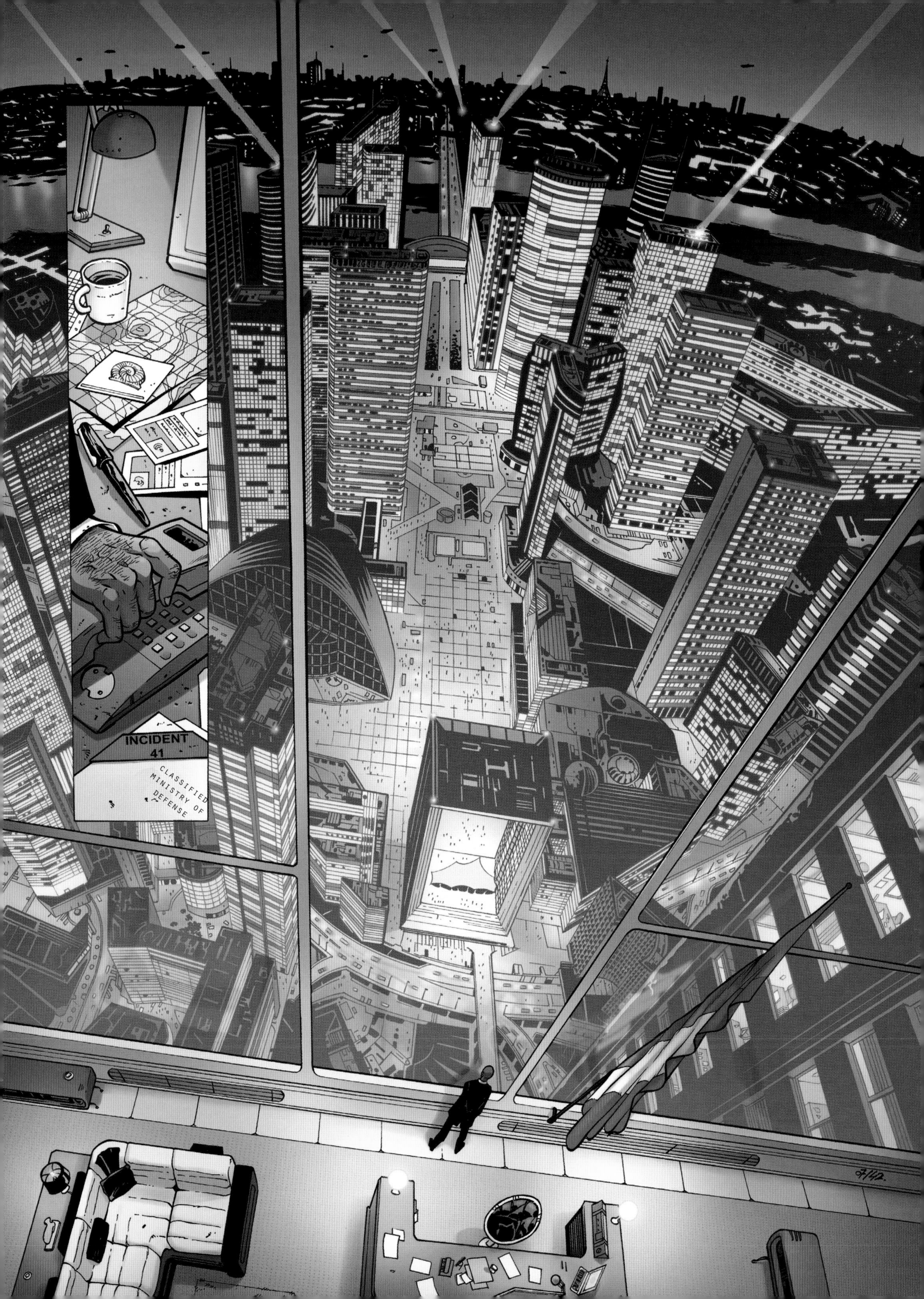
INCIDENT
41
CLASSIFIED
MINISTRY OF
DEFENSE

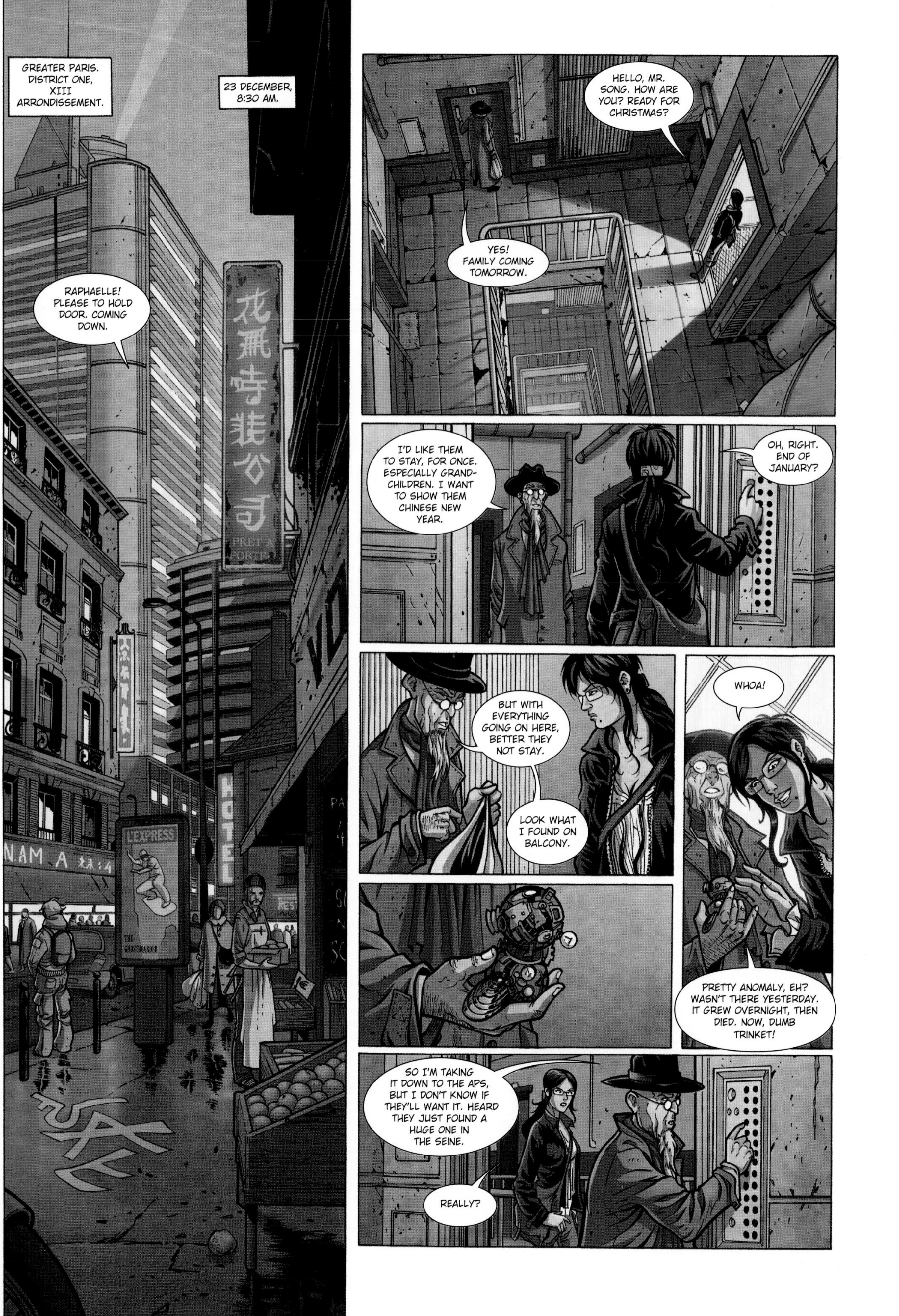
GREATER PARIS. DISTRICT ONE, XIII ARRONDISSEMENT.
23 DECEMBER, 8:30 AM.
RAPHAELLE! PLEASE TO HOLD DOOR. COMING DOWN.
PRET A PORTER
HOTEL
L'EXPRESS
THE GHOSTBOARDER
HELLO, MR. SONG. HOW ARE YOU? READY FOR CHRISTMAS?
YES! FAMILY COMING TOMORROW.
I'D LIKE THEM TO STAY, FOR ONCE. ESPECIALLY GRAND-CHILDREN. I WANT TO SHOW THEM CHINESE NEW YEAR.
OH, RIGHT. END OF JANUARY?
BUT WITH EVERYTHING GOING ON HERE, BETTER THEY NOT STAY.
LOOK WHAT I FOUND ON BALCONY.
WHOA!
PRETTY ANOMALY, EH? WASN'T THERE YESTERDAY. IT GREW OVERNIGHT, THEN DIED. NOW, DUMB TRINKET!
SO I'M TAKING IT DOWN TO THE APS, BUT I DON'T KNOW IF THEY'LL WANT IT. HEARD THEY JUST FOUND A HUGE ONE IN THE SEINE.
REALLY?

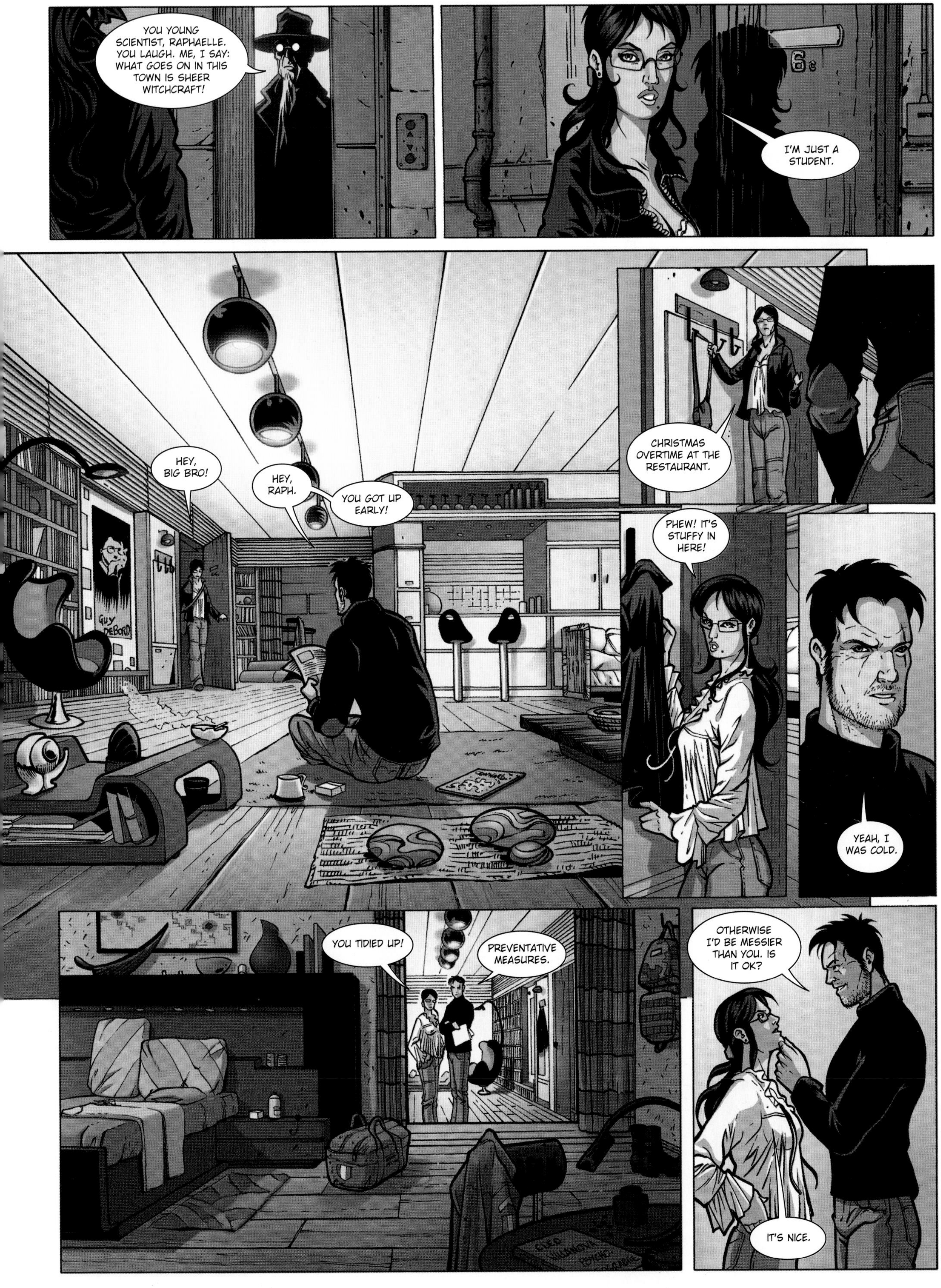

YOU YOUNG SCIENTIST, RAPHAELLE. YOU LAUGH. ME, I SAY: WHAT GOES ON IN THIS TOWN IS SHEER WITCHCRAFT!
I'M JUST A STUDENT.
HEY, BIG BRO!
HEY, RAPH.
YOU GOT UP EARLY!
GUY DEBORD
CHRISTMAS OVERTIME AT THE RESTAURANT.
PHEW! IT'S STUFFY IN HERE!
YEAH, I WAS COLD.
YOU TIDIED UP!
PREVENTATIVE MEASURES.
OTHERWISE I'D BE MESSIER THAN YOU. IS IT OK?
IT'S NICE.

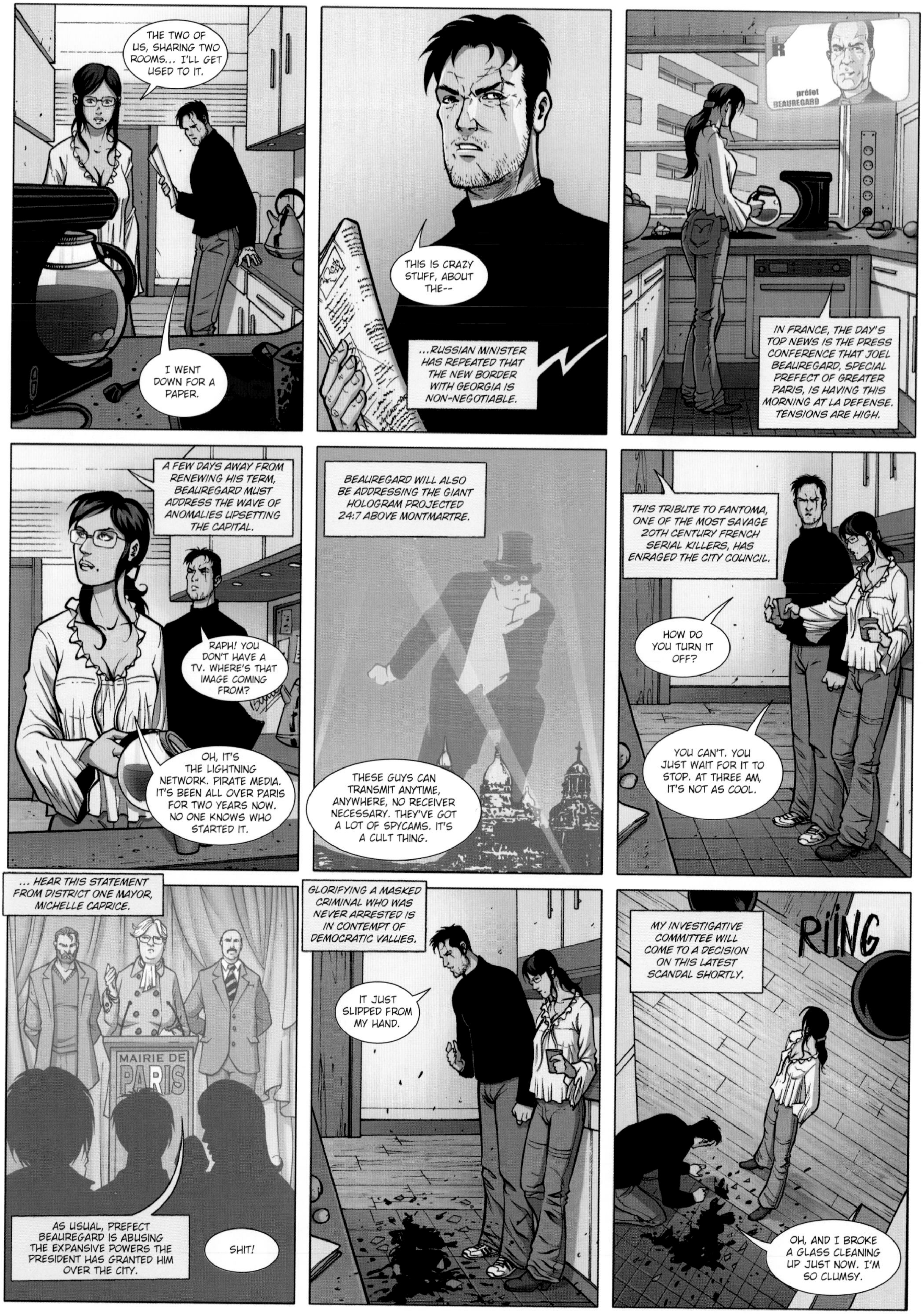
THE TWO OF US, SHARING TWO ROOMS... I'LL GET USED TO IT.
I WENT DOWN FOR A PAPER.
THIS IS CRAZY STUFF, ABOUT THE--
...RUSSIAN MINISTER HAS REPEATED THAT THE NEW BORDER WITH GEORGIA IS NON-NEGOTIABLE.
préfet BEAUREGARD
IN FRANCE, THE DAY'S TOP NEWS IS THE PRESS CONFERENCE THAT JOEL BEAUREGARD, SPECIAL PREFECT OF GREATER PARIS, IS HAVING THIS MORNING AT LA DEFENSE. TENSIONS ARE HIGH.
A FEW DAYS AWAY FROM RENEWING HIS TERM, BEAUREGARD MUST ADDRESS THE WAVE OF ANOMALIES UPSETTING THE CAPITAL.
RAPH! YOU DON'T HAVE A TV. WHERE'S THAT IMAGE COMING FROM?
OH, IT'S THE LIGHTNING NETWORK. PIRATE MEDIA. IT'S BEEN ALL OVER PARIS FOR TWO YEARS NOW. NO ONE KNOWS WHO STARTED IT.
BEAUREGARD WILL ALSO BE ADDRESSING THE GIANT HOLOGRAM PROJECTED 24:7 ABOVE MONTMARTRE.
THESE GUYS CAN TRANSMIT ANYTIME, ANYWHERE, NO RECEIVER NECESSARY. THEY'VE GOT A LOT OF SPYCAMS. IT'S A CULT THING.
THIS TRIBUTE TO FANTOMA, ONE OF THE MOST SAVAGE 20TH CENTURY FRENCH SERIAL KILLERS, HAS ENRAGED THE CITY COUNCIL.
HOW DO YOU TURN IT OFF?
YOU CAN'T. YOU JUST WAIT FOR IT TO STOP. AT THREE AM, IT'S NOT AS COOL.
... HEAR THIS STATEMENT FROM DISTRICT ONE MAYOR, MICHELLE CAPRICE.
MAIRIE DE PARIS
AS USUAL, PREFECT BEAUREGARD IS ABUSING THE EXPANSIVE POWERS THE PRESIDENT HAS GRANTED HIM OVER THE CITY.
SHIT!
GLORIFYING A MASKED CRIMINAL WHO WAS NEVER ARRESTED IS IN CONTEMPT OF DEMOCRATIC VALUES.
IT JUST SLIPPED FROM MY HAND.
MY INVESTIGATIVE COMMITTEE WILL COME TO A DECISION ON THIS LATEST SCANDAL SHORTLY.
RIING
OH, AND I BROKE A GLASS CLEANING UP JUST NOW. I'M SO CLUMSY.

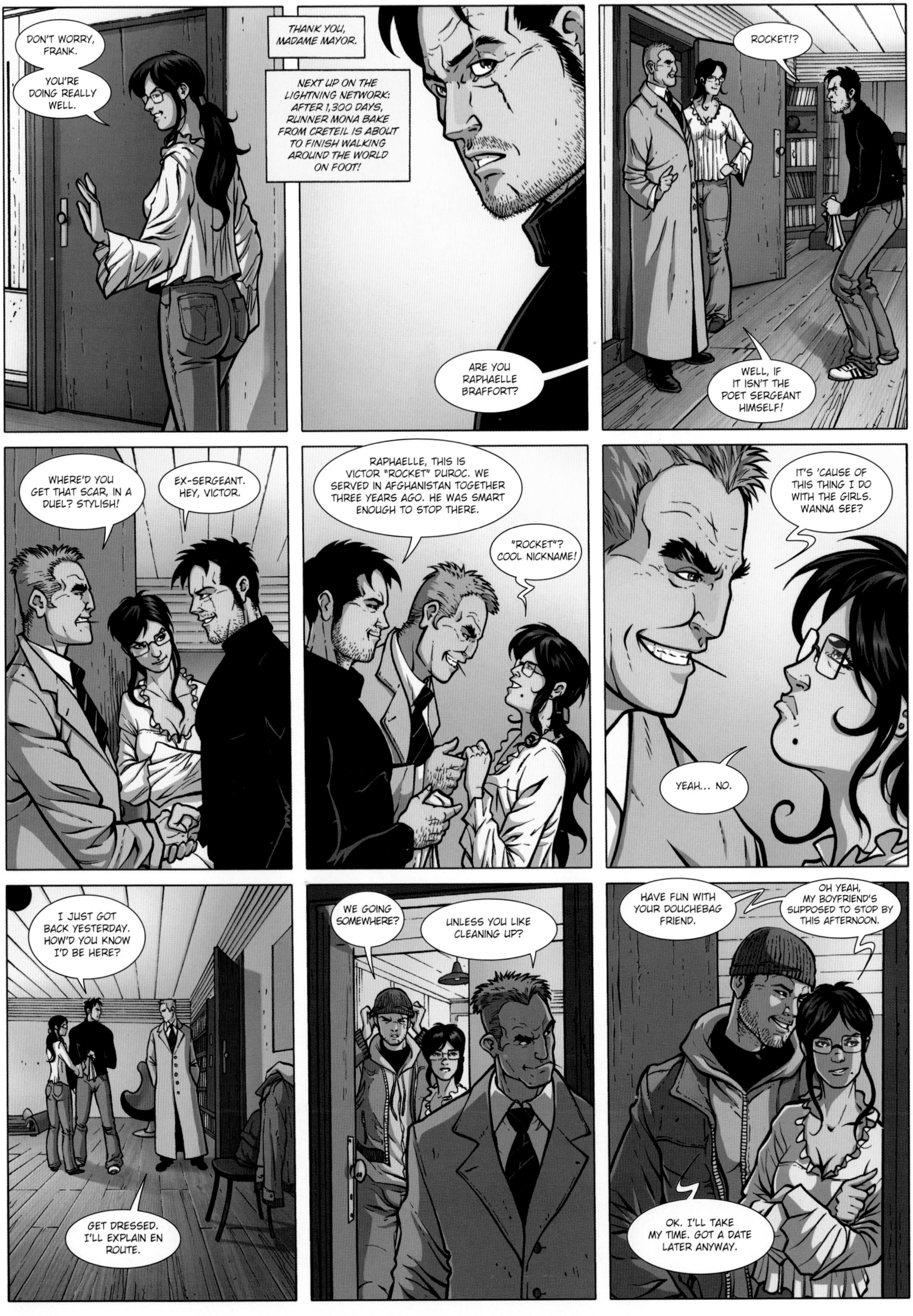
DON'T WORRY, FRANK.
YOU'RE DOING REALLY WELL.
THANK YOU, MADAME MAYOR.
NEXT UP ON THE LIGHTNING NETWORK: AFTER 1,300 DAYS, RUNNER MONA BAKE FROM CRETEIL IS ABOUT TO FINISH WALKING AROUND THE WORLD ON FOOT!
ARE YOU RAPHAELLE BRAFFORT?
ROCKET!?
WELL, IF IT ISN'T THE POET SERGEANT HIMSELF!
WHERE'D YOU GET THAT SCAR, IN A DUEL? STYLISH!
EX-SERGEANT. HEY, VICTOR.
RAPHAELLE, THIS IS VICTOR "ROCKET" DUROC. WE SERVED IN AFGHANISTAN TOGETHER THREE YEARS AGO. HE WAS SMART ENOUGH TO STOP THERE.
"ROCKET"? COOL NICKNAME!
IT'S 'CAUSE OF THIS THING I DO WITH THE GIRLS. WANNA SEE?
YEAH... NO.
I JUST GOT BACK YESTERDAY. HOW'D YOU KNOW I'D BE HERE?
GET DRESSED. I'LL EXPLAIN EN ROUTE.
WE GOING SOMEWHERE?
UNLESS YOU LIKE CLEANING UP?
HAVE FUN WITH YOUR DOUCHEBAG FRIEND.
OH YEAH, MY BOYFRIEND'S SUPPOSED TO STOP BY THIS AFTERNOON.
OK. I'LL TAKE MY TIME. GOT A DATE LATER ANYWAY.

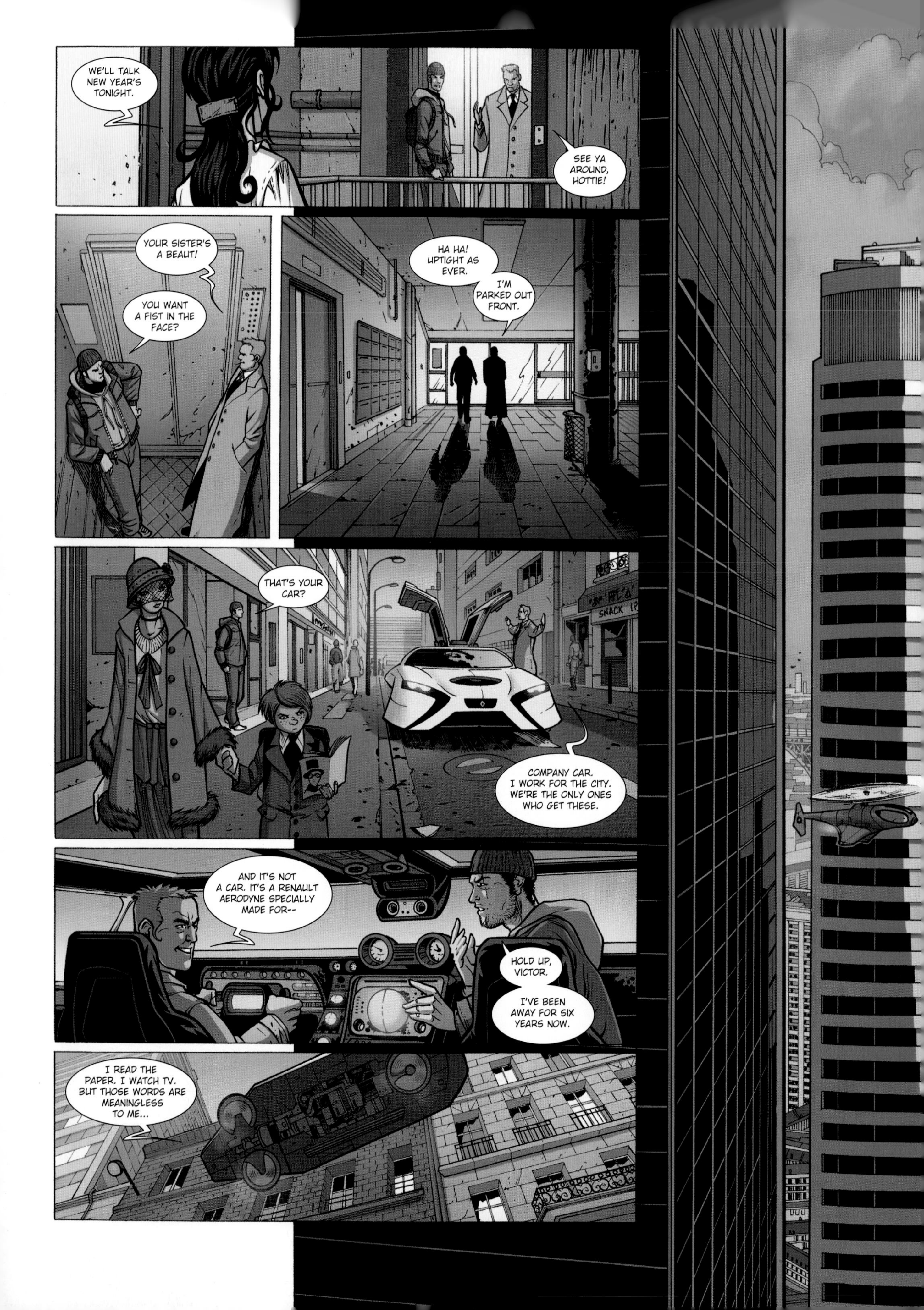

WE'LL TALK NEW YEAR'S TONIGHT.
SEE YA AROUND, HOTTIE!
YOUR SISTER'S A BEAUT!
YOU WANT A FIST IN THE FACE?
HA HA! UPTIGHT AS EVER.
I'M PARKED OUT FRONT.
THAT'S YOUR CAR?
COMPANY CAR. I WORK FOR THE CITY. WE'RE THE ONLY ONES WHO GET THESE.
SNACK
AND IT'S NOT A CAR. IT'S A RENAULT AERODYNE SPECIALLY MADE FOR--
HOLD UP, VICTOR.
I'VE BEEN AWAY FOR SIX YEARS NOW.
I READ THE PAPER. I WATCH TV. BUT THOSE WORDS ARE MEANINGLESS TO ME...

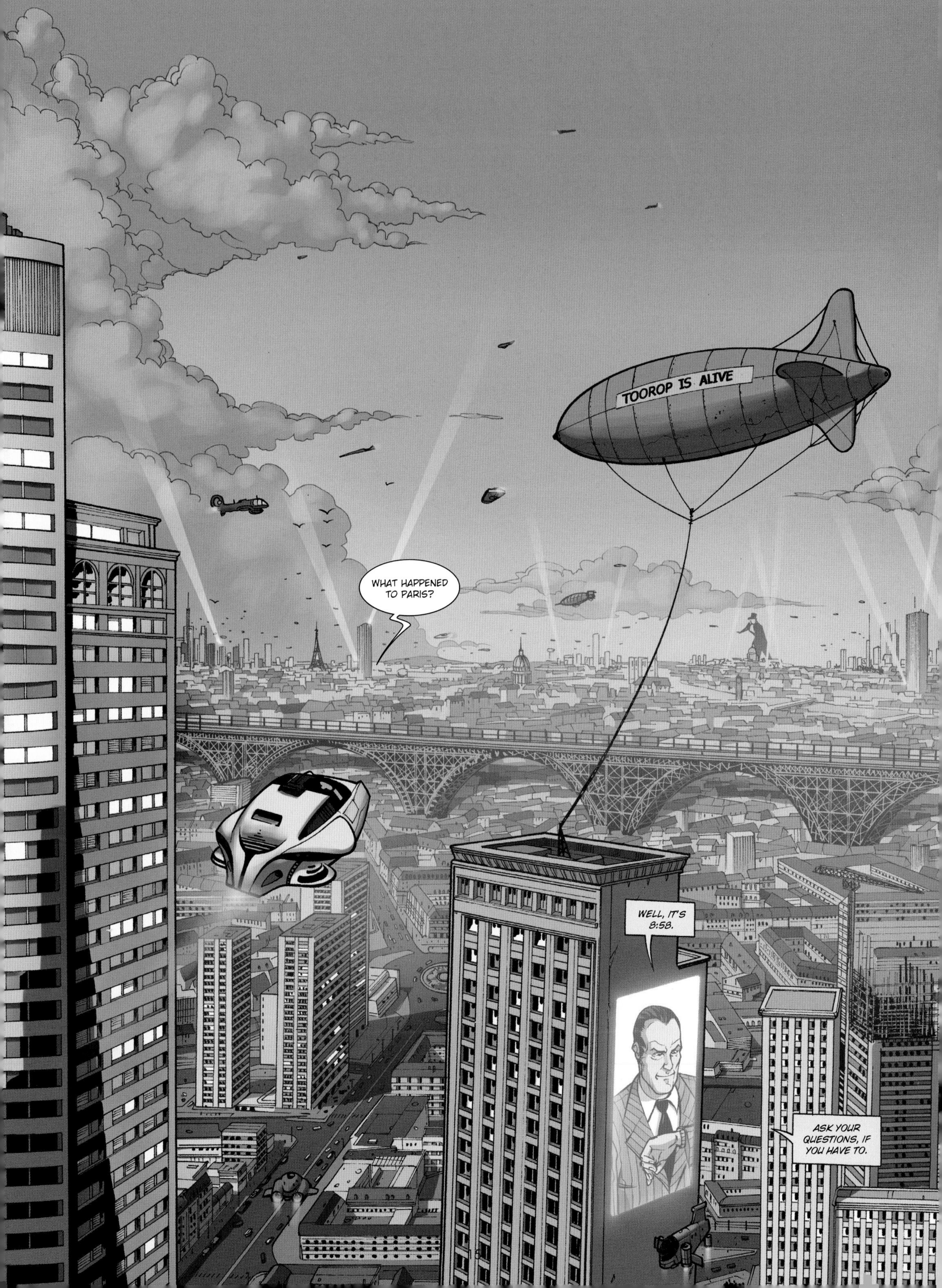
TOOROP IS ALIVE
WHAT HAPPENED TO PARIS?
WELL, IT'S 8:58.
ASK YOUR QUESTIONS, IF YOU HAVE TO.

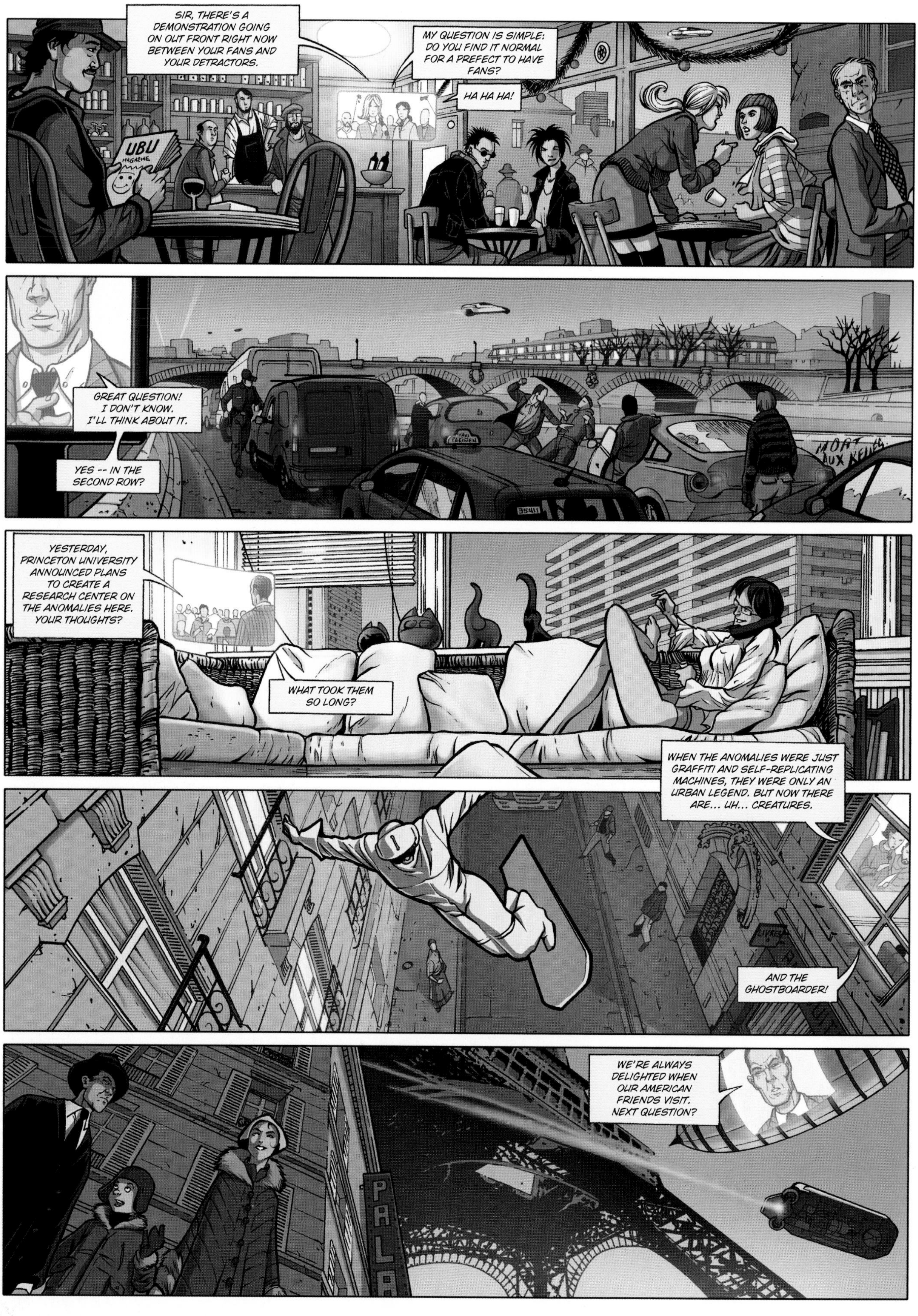
SIR, THERE'S A DEMONSTRATION GOING ON OUT FRONT RIGHT NOW BETWEEN YOUR FANS AND YOUR DETRACTORS.
MY QUESTION IS SIMPLE: DO YOU FIND IT NORMAL FOR A PREFECT TO HAVE FANS?
HA HA HA!
UBU
GREAT QUESTION! I DON'T KNOW. I'LL THINK ABOUT IT.
YES -- IN THE SECOND ROW?
MORT AUX KEUFS
YESTERDAY, PRINCETON UNIVERSITY ANNOUNCED PLANS TO CREATE A RESEARCH CENTER ON THE ANOMALIES HERE. YOUR THOUGHTS?
WHAT TOOK THEM SO LONG?
WHEN THE ANOMALIES WERE JUST GRAFFITI AND SELF-REPLICATING MACHINES, THEY WERE ONLY AN URBAN LEGEND. BUT NOW THERE ARE... UH... CREATURES.
LIVRES
AND THE GHOSTBOARDER!
WE'RE ALWAYS DELIGHTED WHEN OUR AMERICAN FRIENDS VISIT. NEXT QUESTION?
PALA

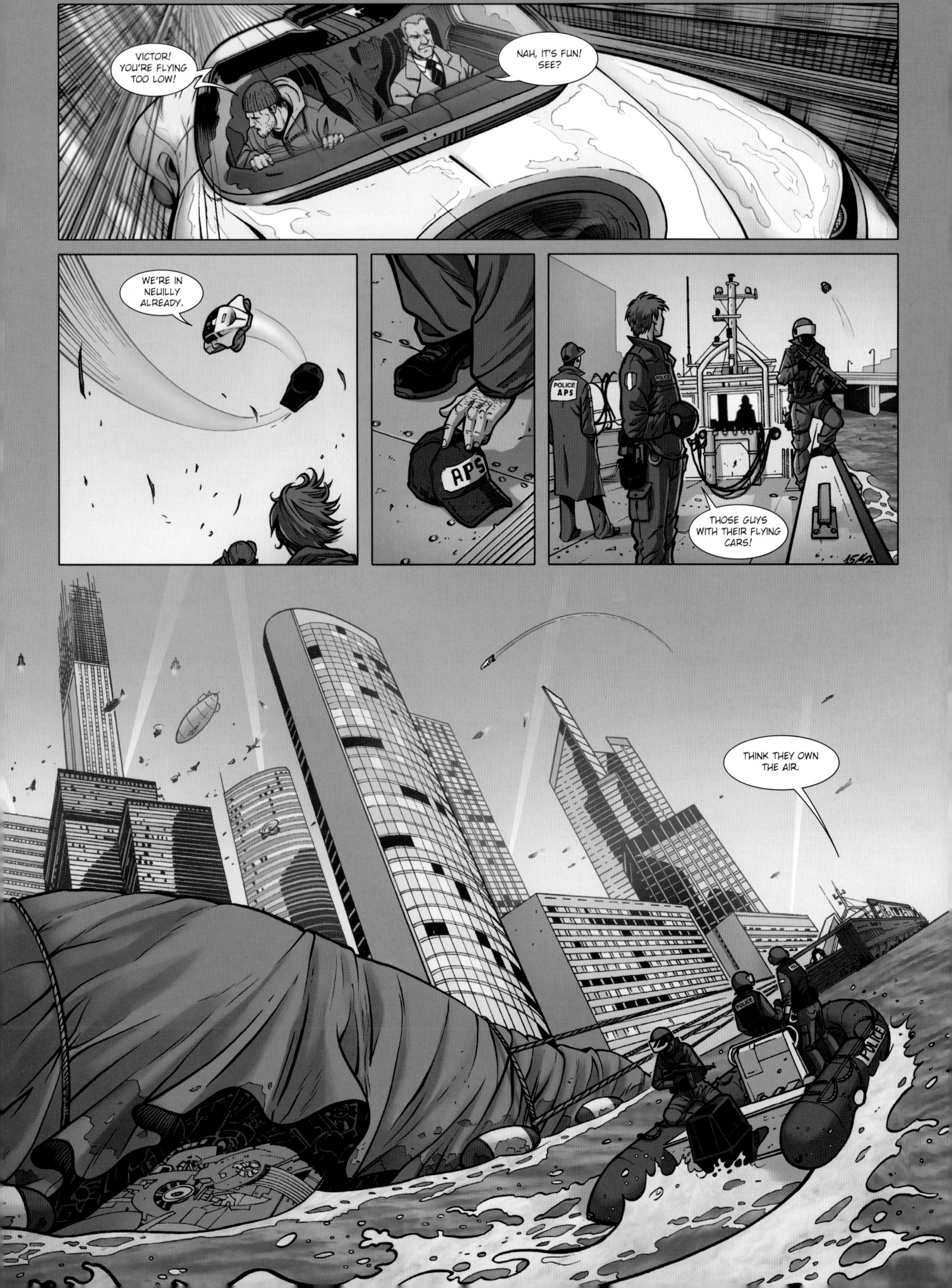
VICTOR! YOU'RE FLYING TOO LOW!
NAH, IT'S FUN! SEE?
WE'RE IN NEUILLY ALREADY.
APS
POLICE APS
POLICE
THOSE GUYS WITH THEIR FLYING CARS!
THINK THEY OWN THE AIR.
POLICE

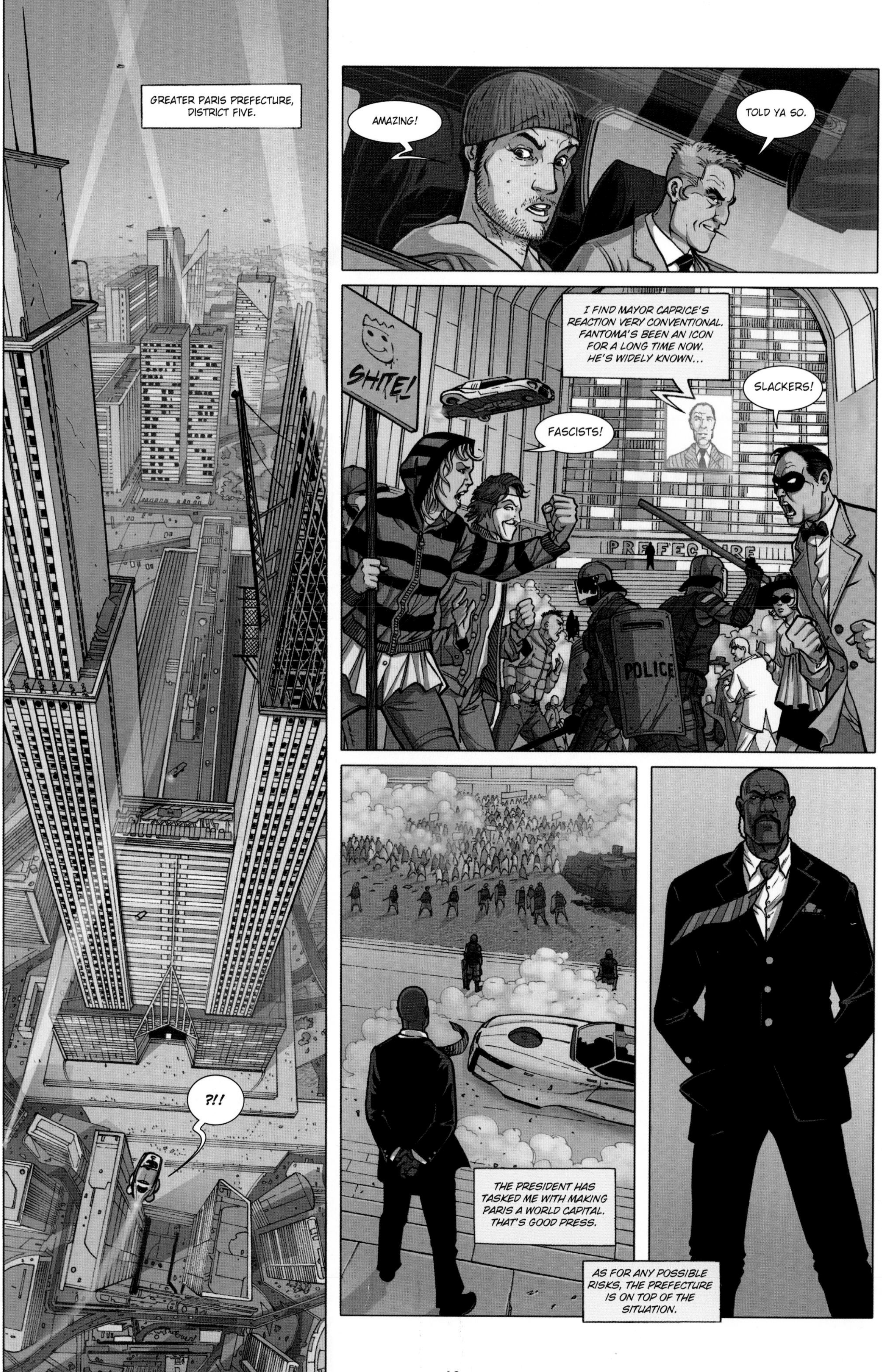
GREATER PARIS PREFECTURE, DISTRICT FIVE.
?!!
AMAZING!
TOLD YA SO.
SHITE!
I FIND MAYOR CAPRICE'S REACTION VERY CONVENTIONAL. FANTOMA'S BEEN AN ICON FOR A LONG TIME NOW. HE'S WIDELY KNOWN...
SLACKERS!
FASCISTS!
PREFECTURE
POLICE
THE PRESIDENT HAS TASKED ME WITH MAKING PARIS A WORLD CAPITAL. THAT'S GOOD PRESS.
AS FOR ANY POSSIBLE RISKS, THE PREFECTURE IS ON TOP OF THE SITUATION.

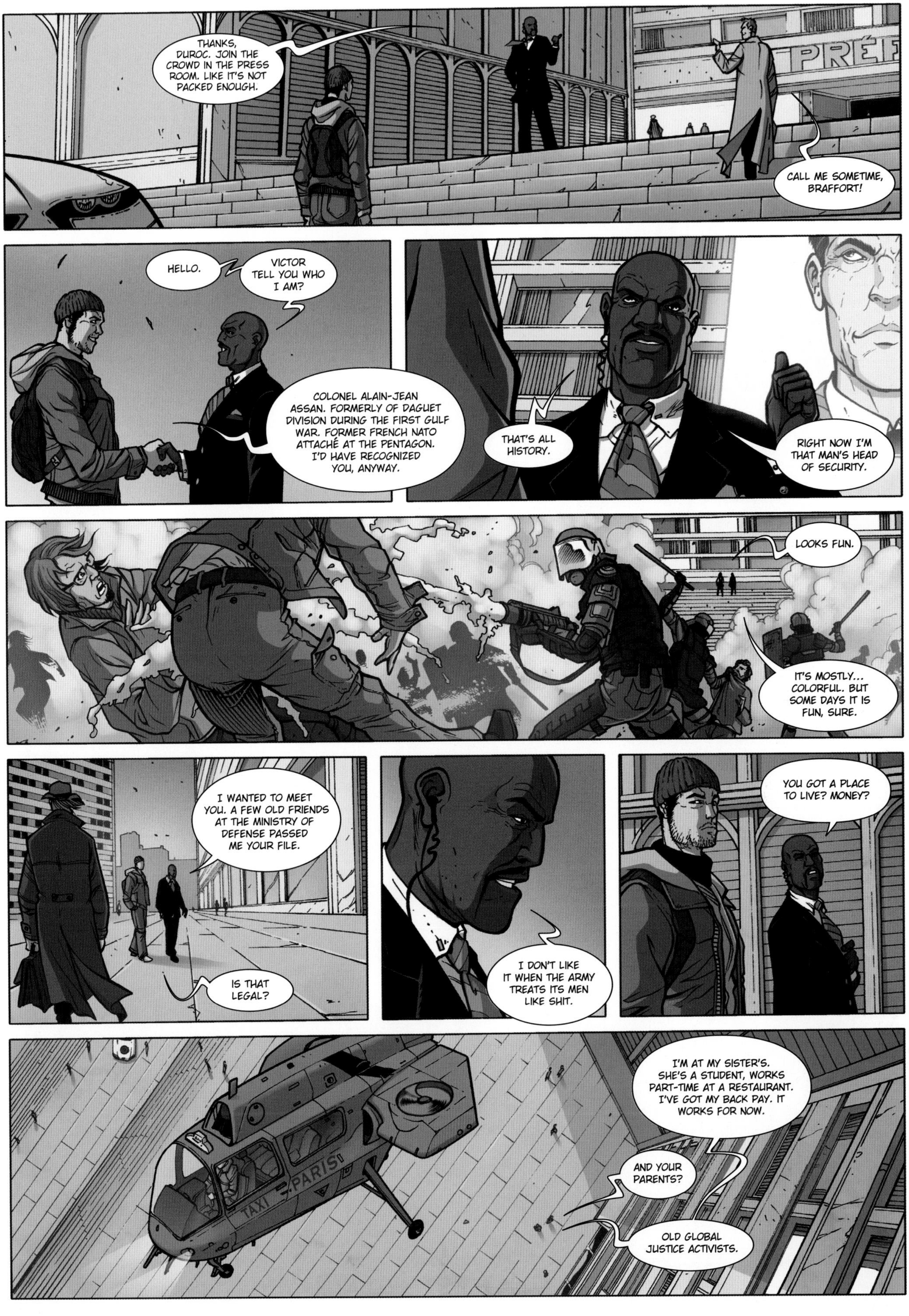
THANKS, DUROC. JOIN THE CROWD IN THE PRESS ROOM. LIKE IT'S NOT PACKED ENOUGH.
PRÉF
CALL ME SOMETIME, BRAFFORT!
HELLO.
VICTOR TELL YOU WHO I AM?
COLONEL ALAIN-JEAN ASSAN. FORMERLY OF DAGUET DIVISION DURING THE FIRST GULF WAR. FORMER FRENCH NATO ATTACHÉ AT THE PENTAGON. I'D HAVE RECOGNIZED YOU, ANYWAY.
THAT'S ALL HISTORY.
RIGHT NOW I'M THAT MAN'S HEAD OF SECURITY.
LOOKS FUN.
IT'S MOSTLY... COLORFUL. BUT SOME DAYS IT IS FUN, SURE.
I WANTED TO MEET YOU. A FEW OLD FRIENDS AT THE MINISTRY OF DEFENSE PASSED ME YOUR FILE.
IS THAT LEGAL?
I DON'T LIKE IT WHEN THE ARMY TREATS ITS MEN LIKE SHIT.
YOU GOT A PLACE TO LIVE? MONEY?
I'M AT MY SISTER'S. SHE'S A STUDENT, WORKS PART-TIME AT A RESTAURANT. I'VE GOT MY BACK PAY. IT WORKS FOR NOW.
AND YOUR PARENTS?
OLD GLOBAL JUSTICE ACTIVISTS.
TAXI PARIS

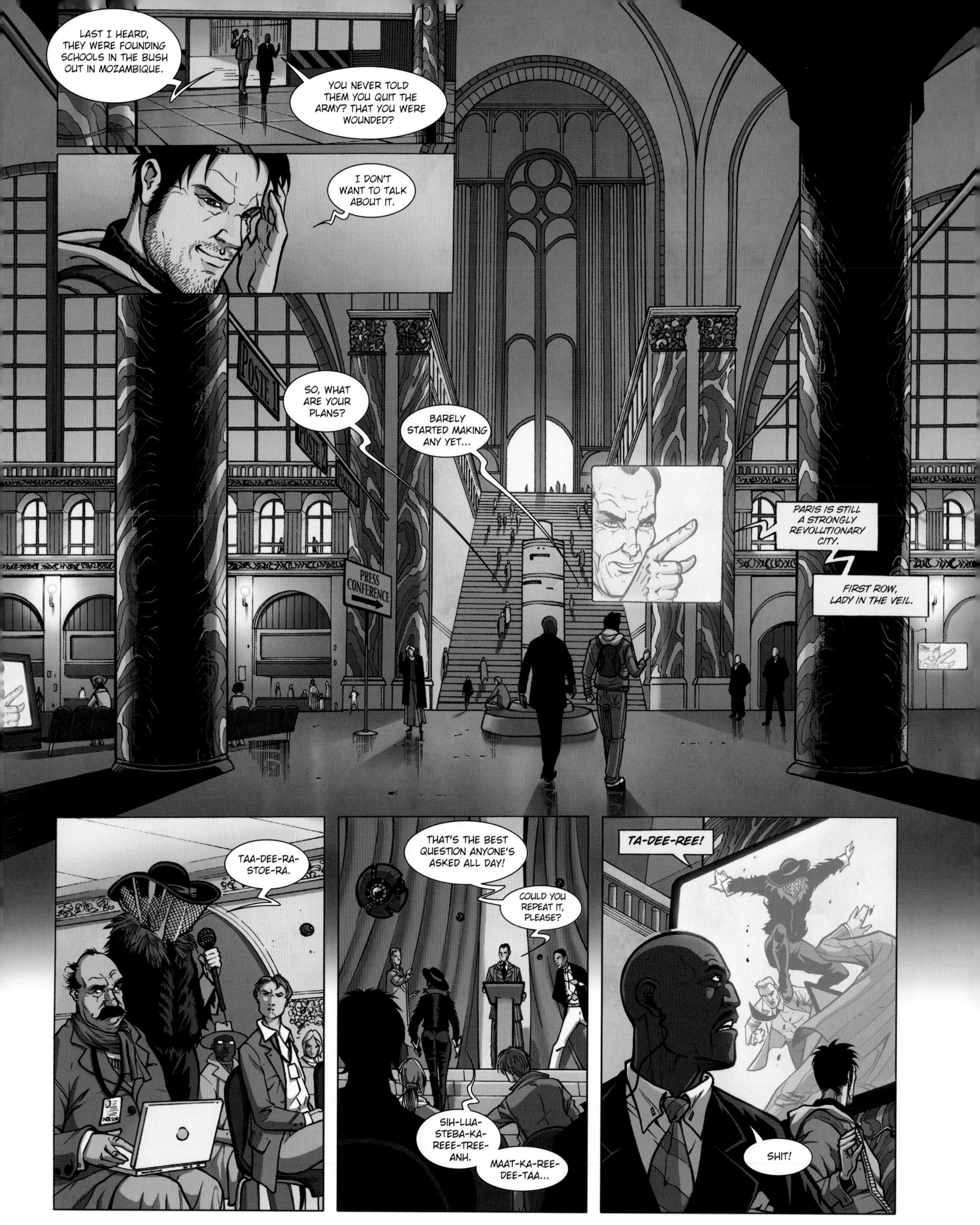
LAST I HEARD, THEY WERE FOUNDING SCHOOLS IN THE BUSH OUT IN MOZAMBIQUE.
YOU NEVER TOLD THEM YOU QUIT THE ARMY? THAT YOU WERE WOUNDED?
I DON'T WANT TO TALK ABOUT IT.
POSTE 1
SO, WHAT ARE YOUR PLANS?
BARELY STARTED MAKING ANY YET...
PRESS CONFERENCE
PARIS IS STILL A STRONGLY REVOLUTIONARY CITY.
FIRST ROW, LADY IN THE VEIL.
TAA-DEE-RA-STOE-RA.
THAT'S THE BEST QUESTION ANYONE'S ASKED ALL DAY!
COULD YOU REPEAT IT, PLEASE?
SIH-LUA-STEBA-KA-REEE-TREE-ANH.
MAAT-KA-REE-DEE-TAA...
TA-DEE-REE!
SHIT!

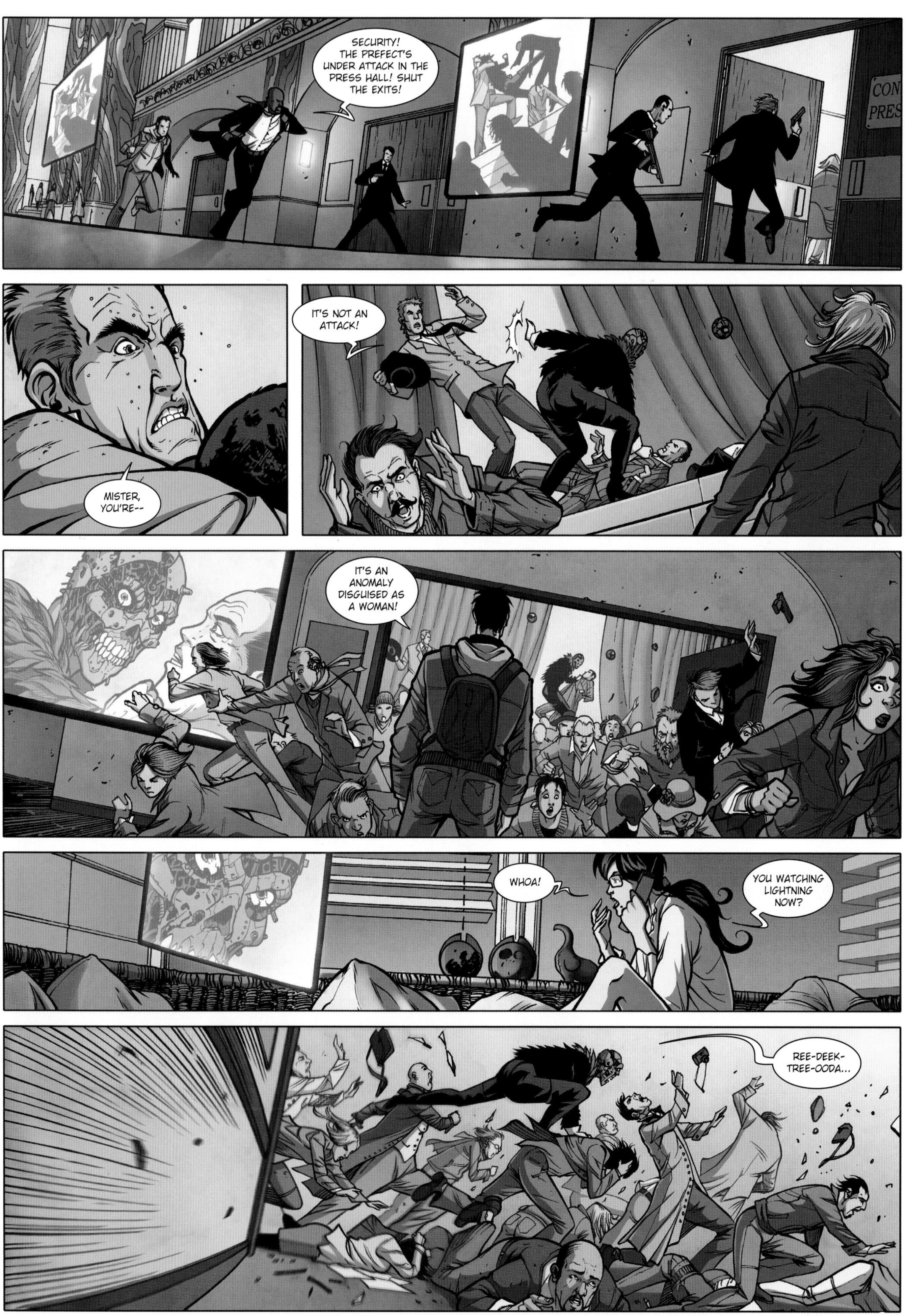
SECURITY! THE PREFECT'S UNDER ATTACK IN THE PRESS HALL! SHUT THE EXITS!
MISTER, YOU'RE--
IT'S NOT AN ATTACK!
IT'S AN ANOMALY DISGUISED AS A WOMAN!
WHOA!
YOU WATCHING LIGHTNING NOW?
REE-DEEK-TREE-OODA...

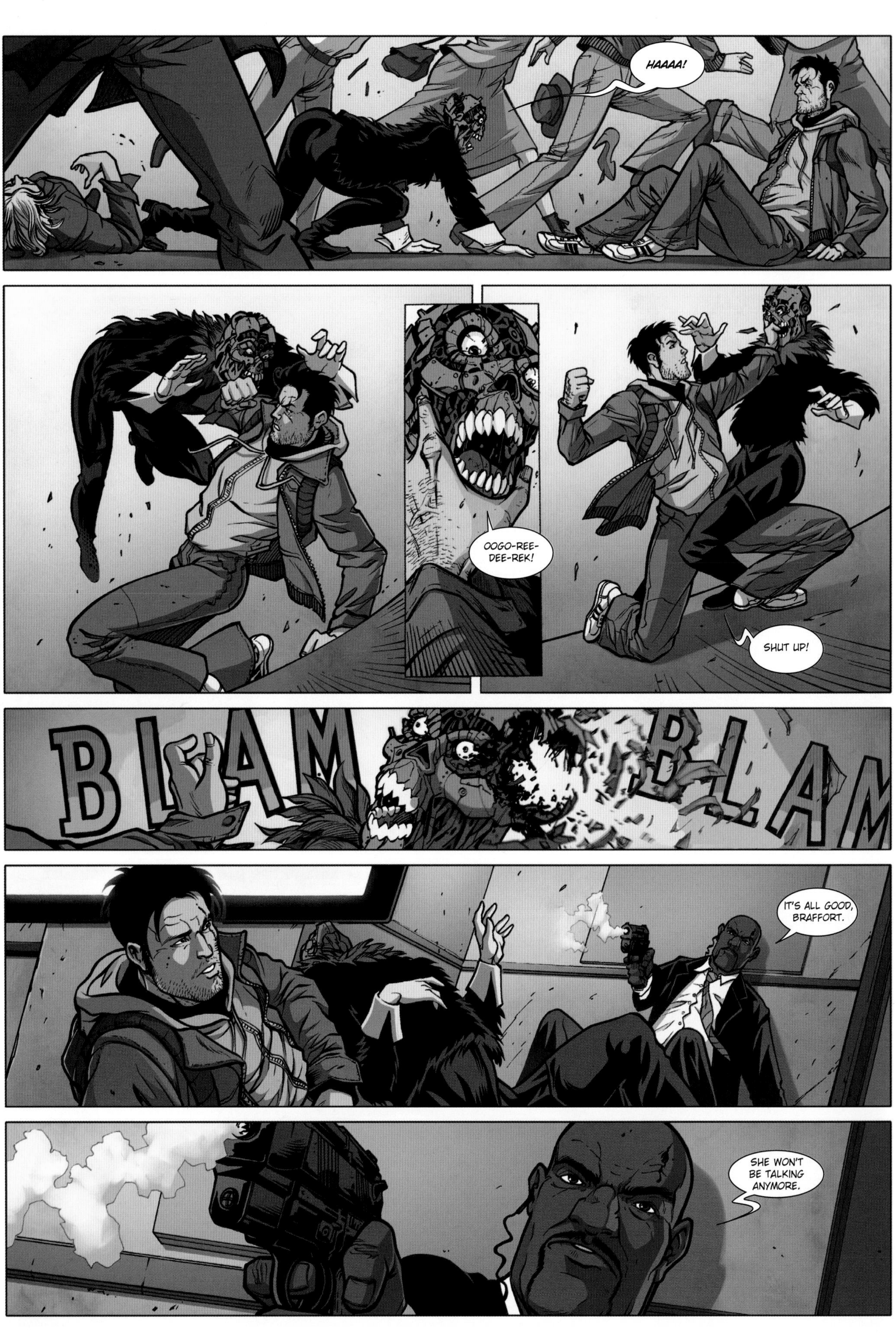
HAAAA!
OOGO-REE-DEE-REK!
SHUT UP!
BLAM
BLAM
IT'S ALL GOOD, BRAFFORT.
SHE WON'T BE TALKING ANYMORE.

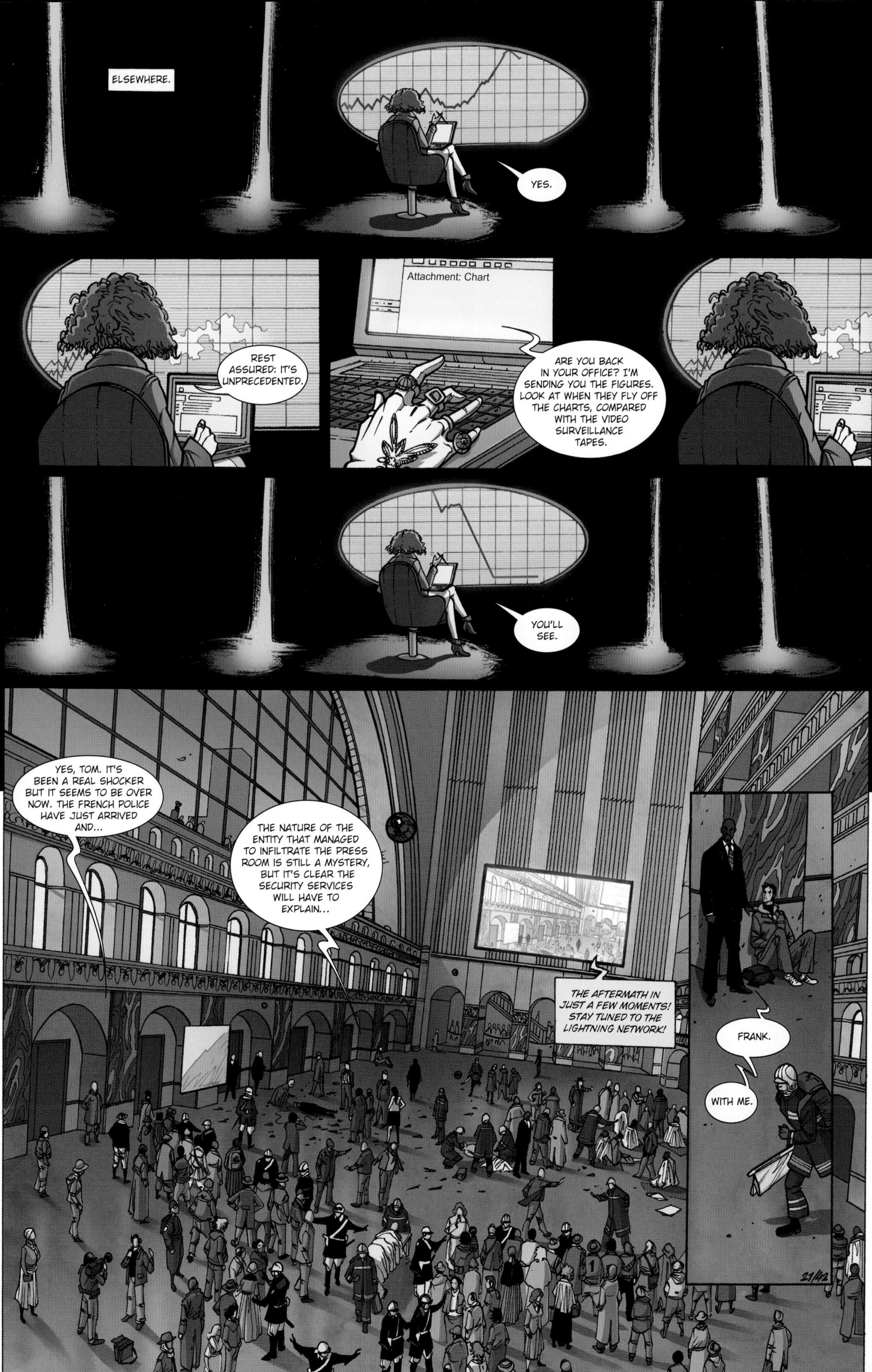
ELSEWHERE.
YES.
REST ASSURED: IT'S UNPRECEDENTED.
Attachment: Chart
ARE YOU BACK IN YOUR OFFICE? I'M SENDING YOU THE FIGURES. LOOK AT WHEN THEY FLY OFF THE CHARTS, COMPARED WITH THE VIDEO SURVEILLANCE TAPES.
YOU'LL SEE.
YES, TOM. IT'S BEEN A REAL SHOCKER BUT IT SEEMS TO BE OVER NOW. THE FRENCH POLICE HAVE JUST ARRIVED AND...
THE NATURE OF THE ENTITY THAT MANAGED TO INFILTRATE THE PRESS ROOM IS STILL A MYSTERY, BUT IT'S CLEAR THE SECURITY SERVICES WILL HAVE TO EXPLAIN...
THE AFTERMATH IN JUST A FEW MOMENTS! STAY TUNED TO THE LIGHTNING NETWORK!
FRANK.
WITH ME.
21/42

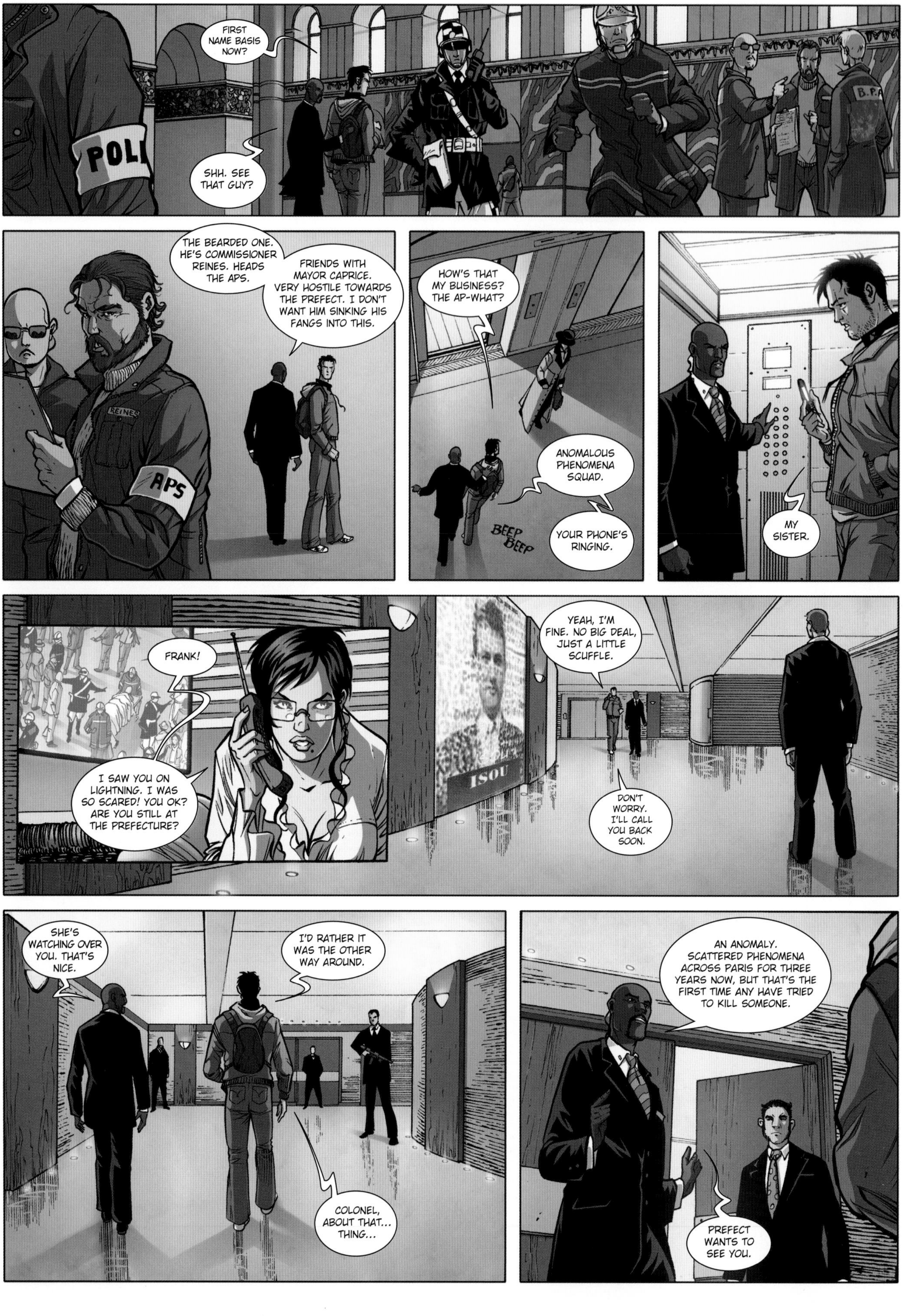
FIRST NAME BASIS NOW?
SHH. SEE THAT GUY?
POLI
THE BEARDED ONE. HE'S COMMISSIONER REINES. HEADS THE APS.
FRIENDS WITH MAYOR CAPRICE. VERY HOSTILE TOWARDS THE PREFECT. I DON'T WANT HIM SINKING HIS FANGS INTO THIS.
REINES
APS
HOW'S THAT MY BUSINESS? THE AP-WHAT?
ANOMALOUS PHENOMENA SQUAD.
YOUR PHONE'S RINGING.
BEEP BEEP
MY SISTER.
FRANK!
I SAW YOU ON LIGHTNING. I WAS SO SCARED! YOU OK? ARE YOU STILL AT THE PREFECTURE?
ISOU
YEAH, I'M FINE. NO BIG DEAL, JUST A LITTLE SCUFFLE.
DON'T WORRY. I'LL CALL YOU BACK SOON.
SHE'S WATCHING OVER YOU. THAT'S NICE.
I'D RATHER IT WAS THE OTHER WAY AROUND.
COLONEL, ABOUT THAT... THING...
AN ANOMALY. SCATTERED PHENOMENA ACROSS PARIS FOR THREE YEARS NOW, BUT THAT'S THE FIRST TIME ANY HAVE TRIED TO KILL SOMEONE.
PREFECT WANTS TO SEE YOU.

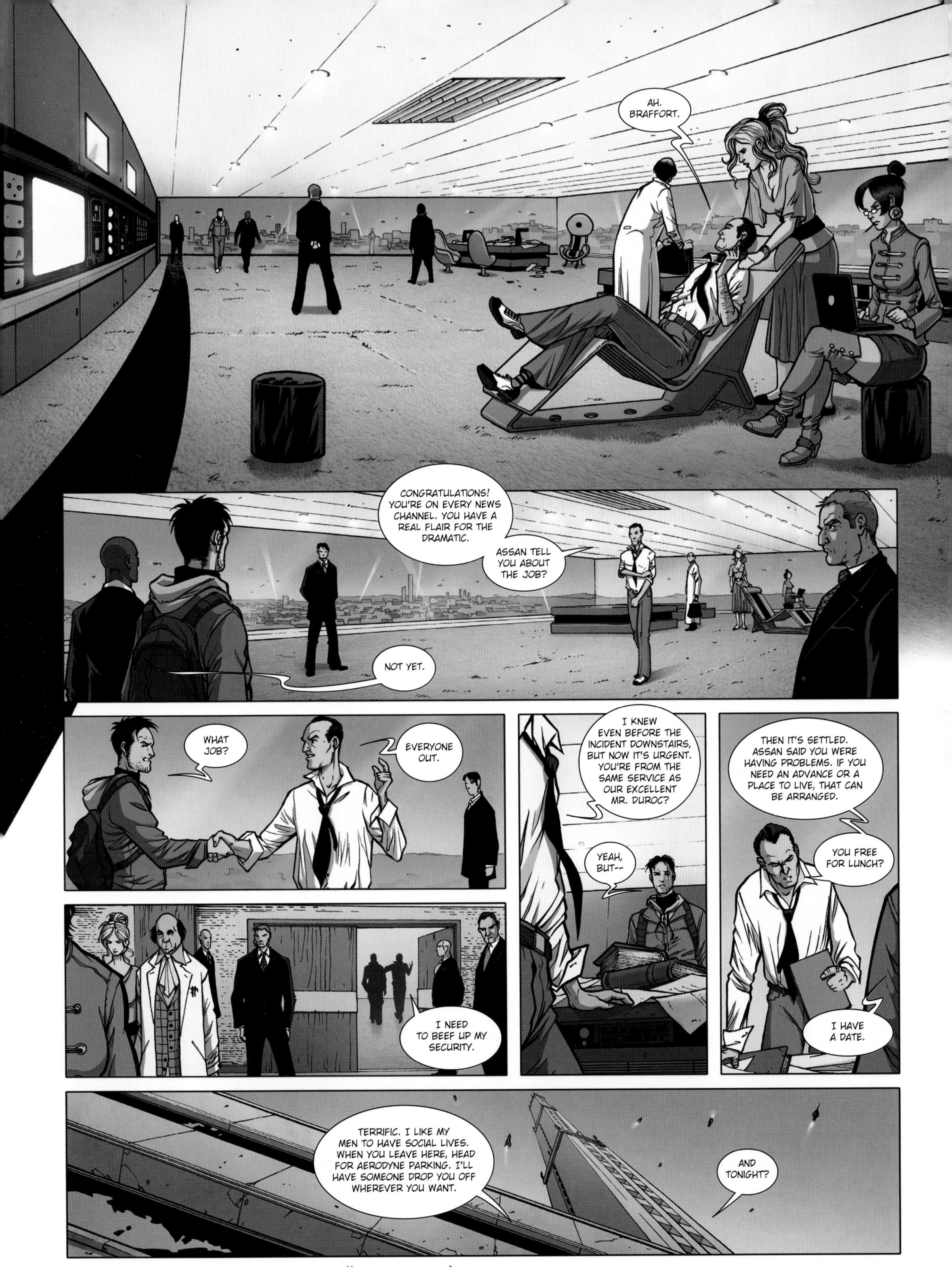
AH. BRAFFORT.
CONGRATULATIONS! YOU'RE ON EVERY NEWS CHANNEL. YOU HAVE A REAL FLAIR FOR THE DRAMATIC.
ASSAN TELL YOU ABOUT THE JOB?
NOT YET.
WHAT JOB?
EVERYONE OUT.
I NEED TO BEEF UP MY SECURITY.
I KNEW EVEN BEFORE THE INCIDENT DOWNSTAIRS, BUT NOW IT'S URGENT. YOU'RE FROM THE SAME SERVICE AS OUR EXCELLENT MR. DUROC?
YEAH, BUT--
THEN IT'S SETTLED. ASSAN SAID YOU WERE HAVING PROBLEMS. IF YOU NEED AN ADVANCE OR A PLACE TO LIVE, THAT CAN BE ARRANGED.
YOU FREE FOR LUNCH?
I HAVE A DATE.
TERRIFIC. I LIKE MY MEN TO HAVE SOCIAL LIVES. WHEN YOU LEAVE HERE, HEAD FOR AERODYNE PARKING. I'LL HAVE SOMEONE DROP YOU OFF WHEREVER YOU WANT.
AND TONIGHT?

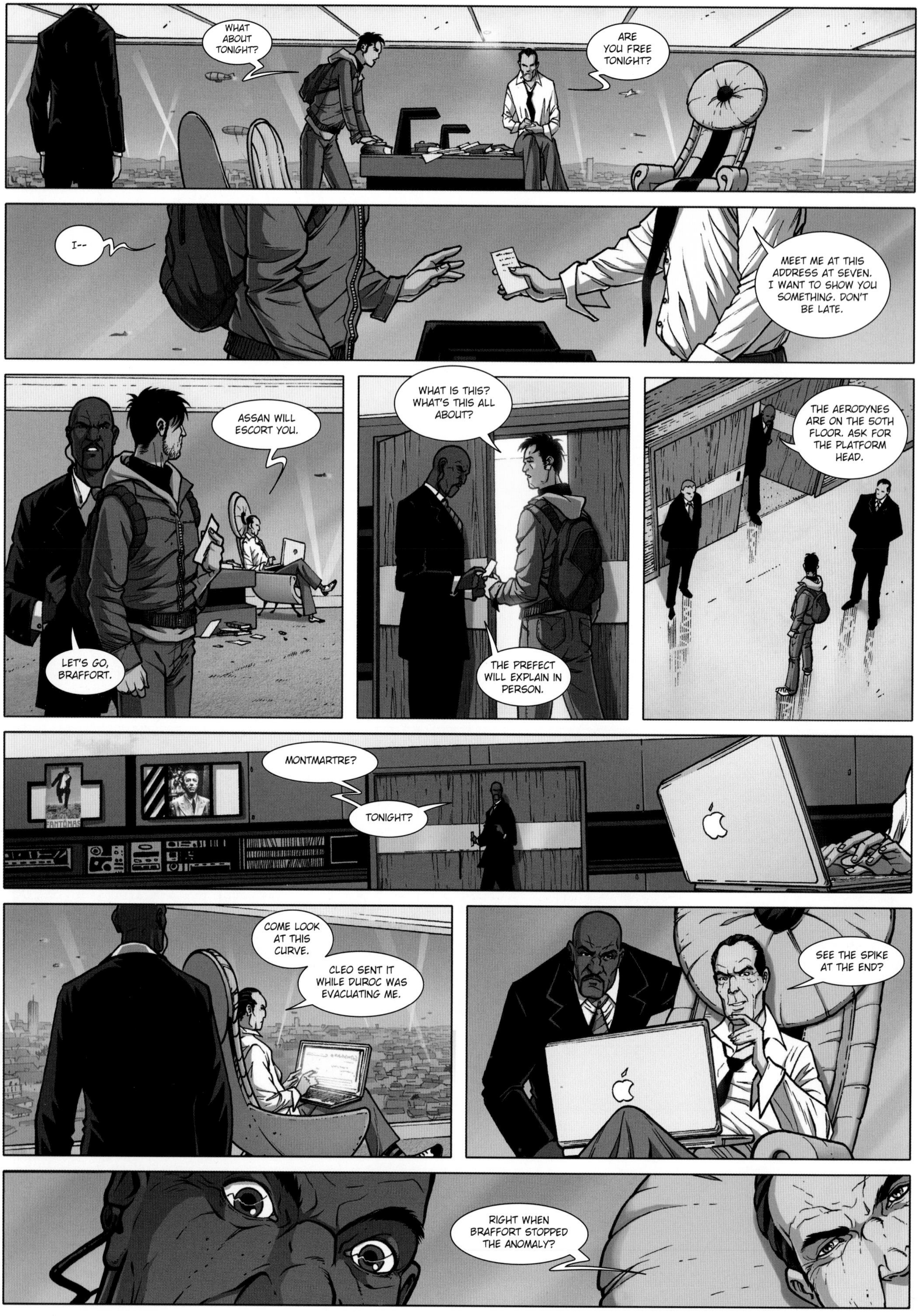

WHAT ABOUT TONIGHT?
ARE YOU FREE TONIGHT?
I--
MEET ME AT THIS ADDRESS AT SEVEN. I WANT TO SHOW YOU SOMETHING. DON'T BE LATE.
ASSAN WILL ESCORT YOU.
LET'S GO, BRAFFORT.
WHAT IS THIS? WHAT'S THIS ALL ABOUT?
THE PREFECT WILL EXPLAIN IN PERSON.
THE AERODYNES ARE ON THE 50TH FLOOR. ASK FOR THE PLATFORM HEAD.
MONTMARTRE?
TONIGHT?
FANTOMAS
COME LOOK AT THIS CURVE.
CLEO SENT IT WHILE DUROC WAS EVACUATING ME.
SEE THE SPIKE AT THE END?
RIGHT WHEN BRAFFORT STOPPED THE ANOMALY?

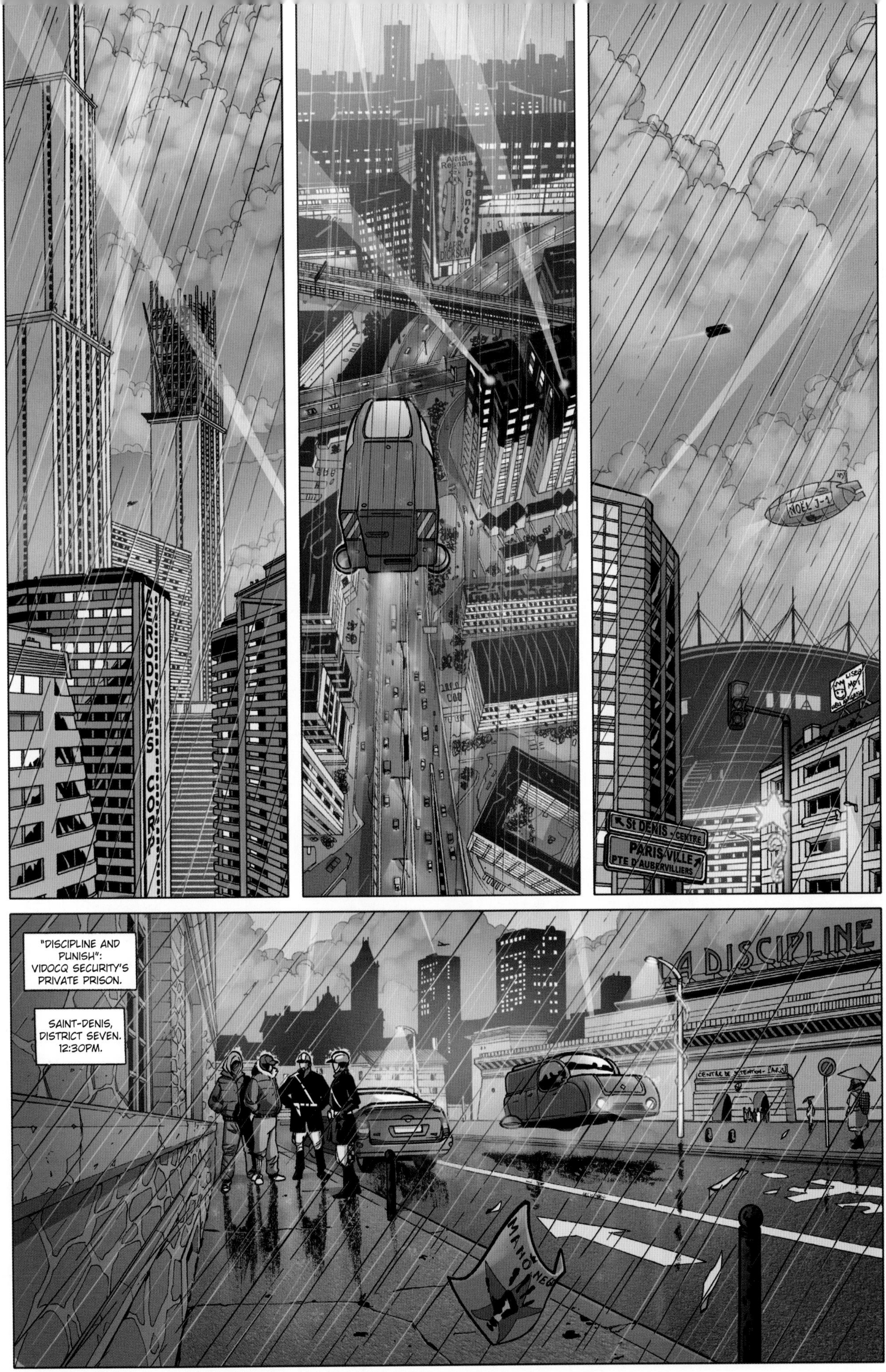
ERODYNES CORP
bientot
NOËL J-1
St DENIS - CENTRE
PARIS-VILLE
PTE D'AUBERVILLIERS
"DISCIPLINE AND PUNISH": VIDOCQ SECURITY'S PRIVATE PRISON.
SAINT-DENIS, DISTRICT SEVEN. 12:30PM.
LA DISCIPLINE

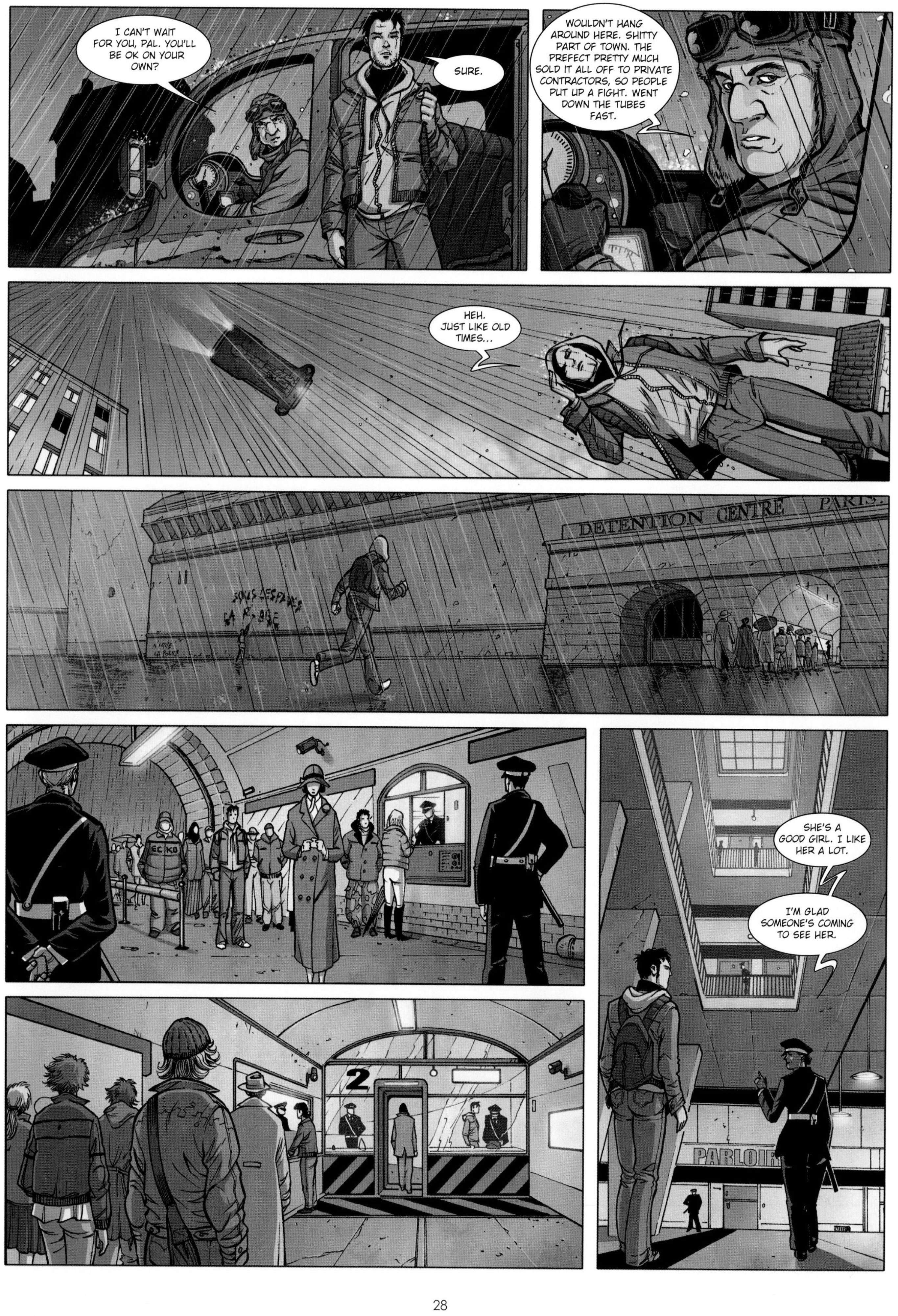
I CAN'T WAIT FOR YOU, PAL. YOU'LL BE OK ON YOUR OWN?
SURE.
WOULDN'T HANG AROUND HERE. SHITTY PART OF TOWN. THE PREFECT PRETTY MUCH SOLD IT ALL OFF TO PRIVATE CONTRACTORS, SO PEOPLE PUT UP A FIGHT. WENT DOWN THE TUBES FAST.
HEH. JUST LIKE OLD TIMES...
DETENTION CENTRE PARIS
SHE'S A GOOD GIRL. I LIKE HER A LOT.
I'M GLAD SOMEONE'S COMING TO SEE HER.
2
PARLOIR

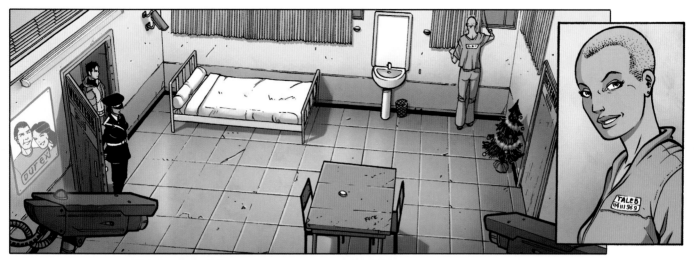

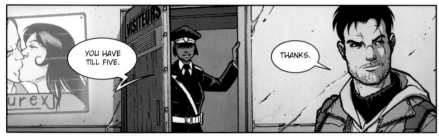

TALEB 114 111 96 9
VISITEURS
YOU HAVE TILL FIVE.
THANKS.
GOOD TO SEE YOU, MEL.
YOU TOO, FRANK.
DÉTENUS
I BROUGHT YOU SOME STUFF.
GAULOISES
Курці помира
CARTON OF CIGS.
THESE ARE LIKE GOLD IN HERE.

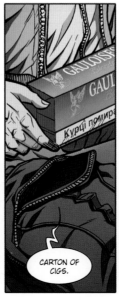

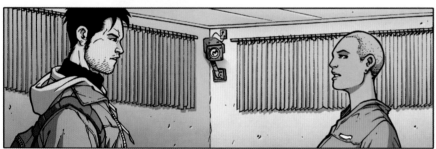

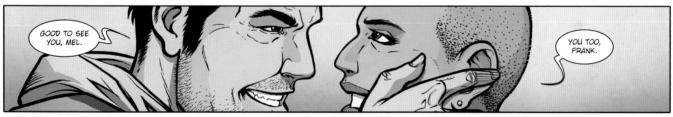

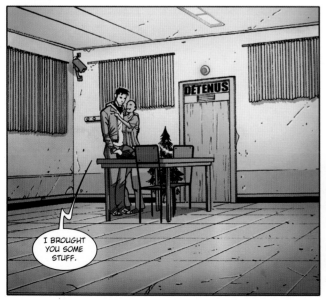

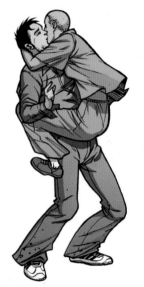

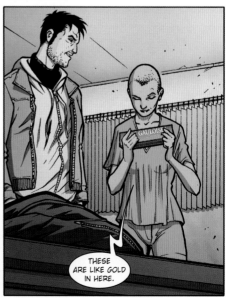

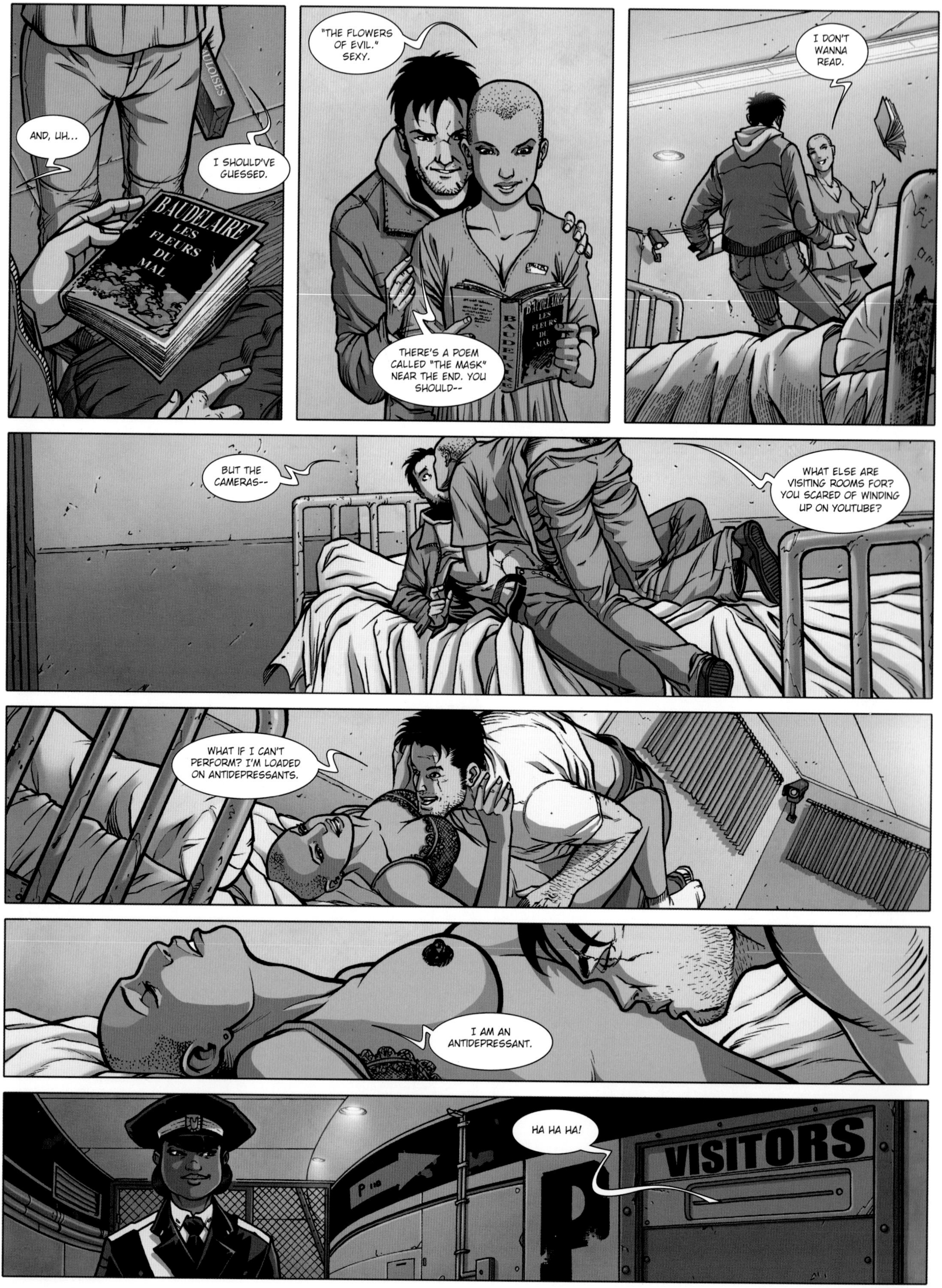
AND, UH...
I SHOULD'VE GUESSED.
BAUDELAIRE LES FLEURS DU MAL
"THE FLOWERS OF EVIL." SEXY.
THERE'S A POEM CALLED "THE MASK" NEAR THE END. YOU SHOULD--
I DON'T WANNA READ.
BUT THE CAMERAS--
WHAT ELSE ARE VISITING ROOMS FOR? YOU SCARED OF WINDING UP ON YOUTUBE?
WHAT IF I CAN'T PERFORM? I'M LOADED ON ANTIDEPRESSANTS.
I AM AN ANTIDEPRESSANT.
HA HA HA!
VISITORS

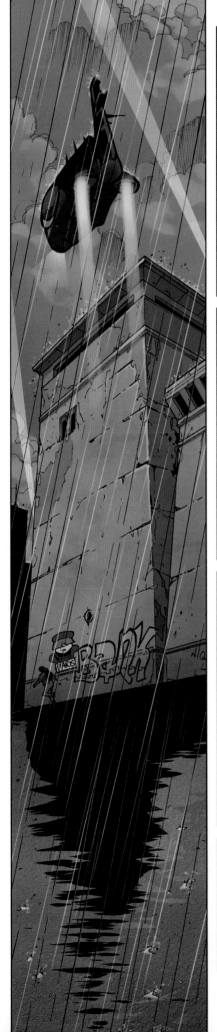

DUMBEST THING I EVER DID.

LEAVING THE ARMY?

NO! WAITING FOR SPILATNY TO GET BACK TO PARIS AND BREAKING HIS FACE.

RIGHT IN FRONT OF HIS HOUSE. HIS WIFE AND KIDS.

MY TRIAL'S IN TWO MONTHS.

DAMN.

HOW 'BOUT YOU? WHAT ARE YOU UP TO?

I'LL STICK AROUND TILL YOUR TRIAL'S OVER. AFTERWARDS, WE'LL SEE.

I DID A LOT OF THINKING IN THE HOSPITAL.

I WANT TO TRY MY LUCK IN THE US, OR CANADA.

AMERICA, IN OTHER WORDS.

RIGHT. AMERICA.

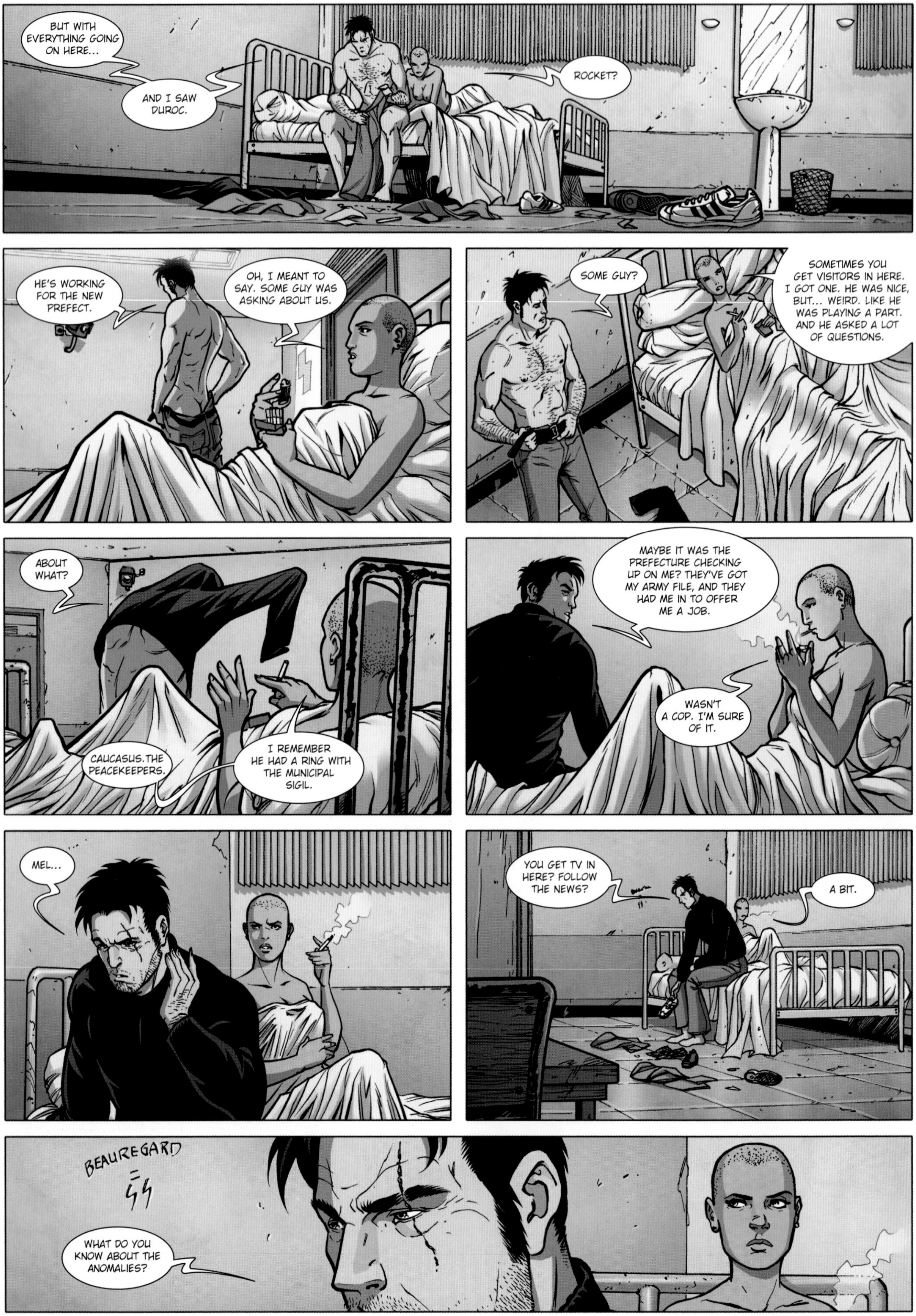
BUT WITH EVERYTHING GOING ON HERE...
AND I SAW DUROC.
ROCKET?
HE'S WORKING FOR THE NEW PREFECT.
OH, I MEANT TO SAY. SOME GUY WAS ASKING ABOUT US.
SOME GUY?
SOMETIMES YOU GET VISITORS IN HERE. I GOT ONE. HE WAS NICE, BUT... WEIRD. LIKE HE WAS PLAYING A PART. AND HE ASKED A LOT OF QUESTIONS.
ABOUT WHAT?
CAUCASUS.THE PEACEKEEPERS.
I REMEMBER HE HAD A RING WITH THE MUNICIPAL SIGIL.
MAYBE IT WAS THE PREFECTURE CHECKING UP ON ME? THEY'VE GOT MY ARMY FILE, AND THEY HAD ME IN TO OFFER ME A JOB.
WASN'T A COP. I'M SURE OF IT.
MEL...
YOU GET TV IN HERE? FOLLOW THE NEWS?
A BIT.
BEAUREGARD
WHAT DO YOU KNOW ABOUT THE ANOMALIES?

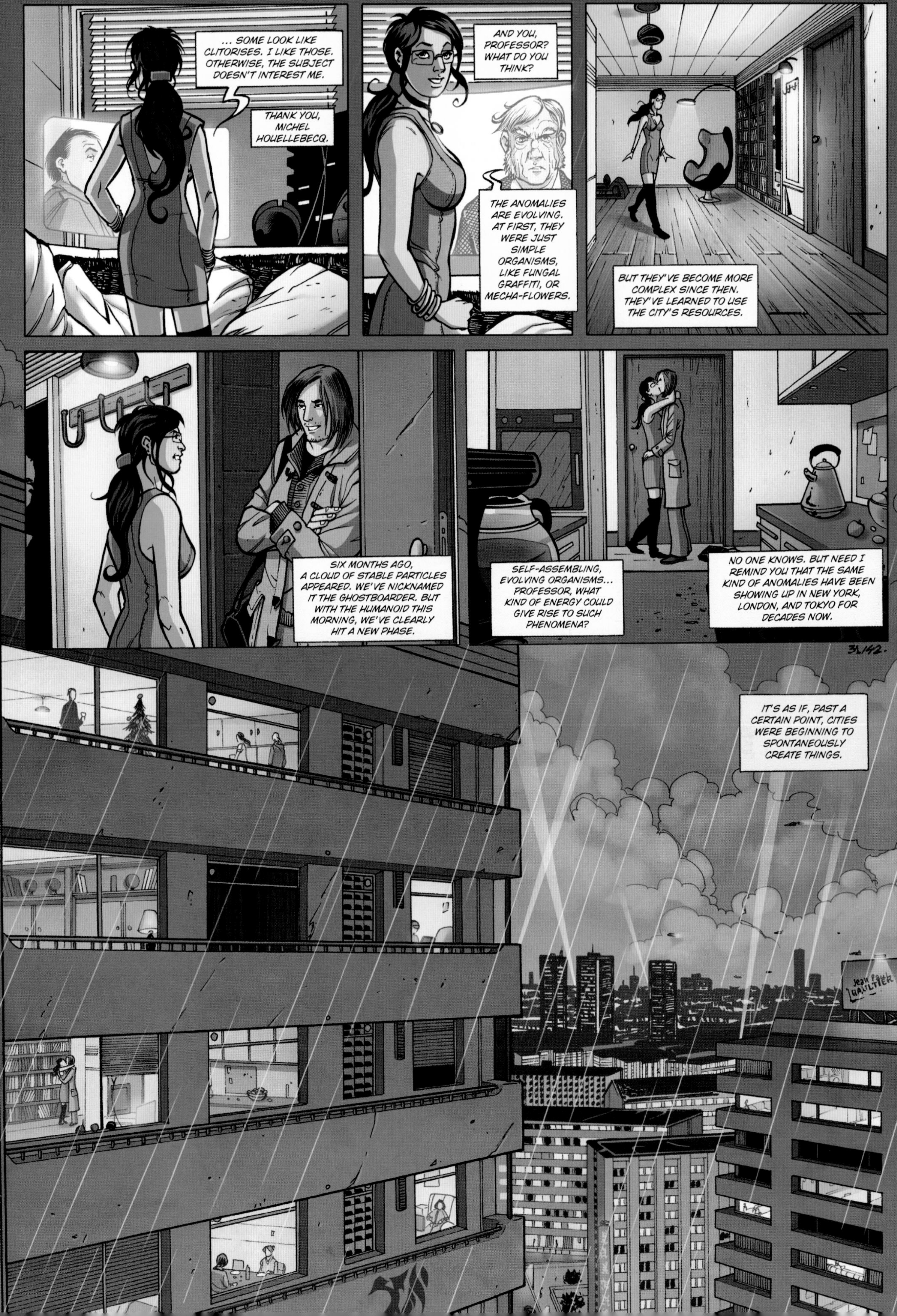
... SOME LOOK LIKE CLITORISES. I LIKE THOSE. OTHERWISE, THE SUBJECT DOESN'T INTEREST ME.
THANK YOU, MICHEL HOUELLEBECQ.
AND YOU, PROFESSOR? WHAT DO YOU THINK?
THE ANOMALIES ARE EVOLVING. AT FIRST, THEY WERE JUST SIMPLE ORGANISMS, LIKE FUNGAL GRAFFITI, OR MECHA-FLOWERS.
BUT THEY'VE BECOME MORE COMPLEX SINCE THEN. THEY'VE LEARNED TO USE THE CITY'S RESOURCES.
SIX MONTHS AGO, A CLOUD OF STABLE PARTICLES APPEARED. WE'VE NICKNAMED IT THE GHOSTBOARDER. BUT WITH THE HUMANOID THIS MORNING, WE'VE CLEARLY HIT A NEW PHASE.
SELF-ASSEMBLING, EVOLVING ORGANISMS... PROFESSOR, WHAT KIND OF ENERGY COULD GIVE RISE TO SUCH PHENOMENA?
NO ONE KNOWS. BUT NEED I REMIND YOU THAT THE SAME KIND OF ANOMALIES HAVE BEEN SHOWING UP IN NEW YORK, LONDON, AND TOKYO FOR DECADES NOW.
IT'S AS IF, PAST A CERTAIN POINT, CITIES WERE BEGINNING TO SPONTANEOUSLY CREATE THINGS.
JEAN PAUL GAULTIER

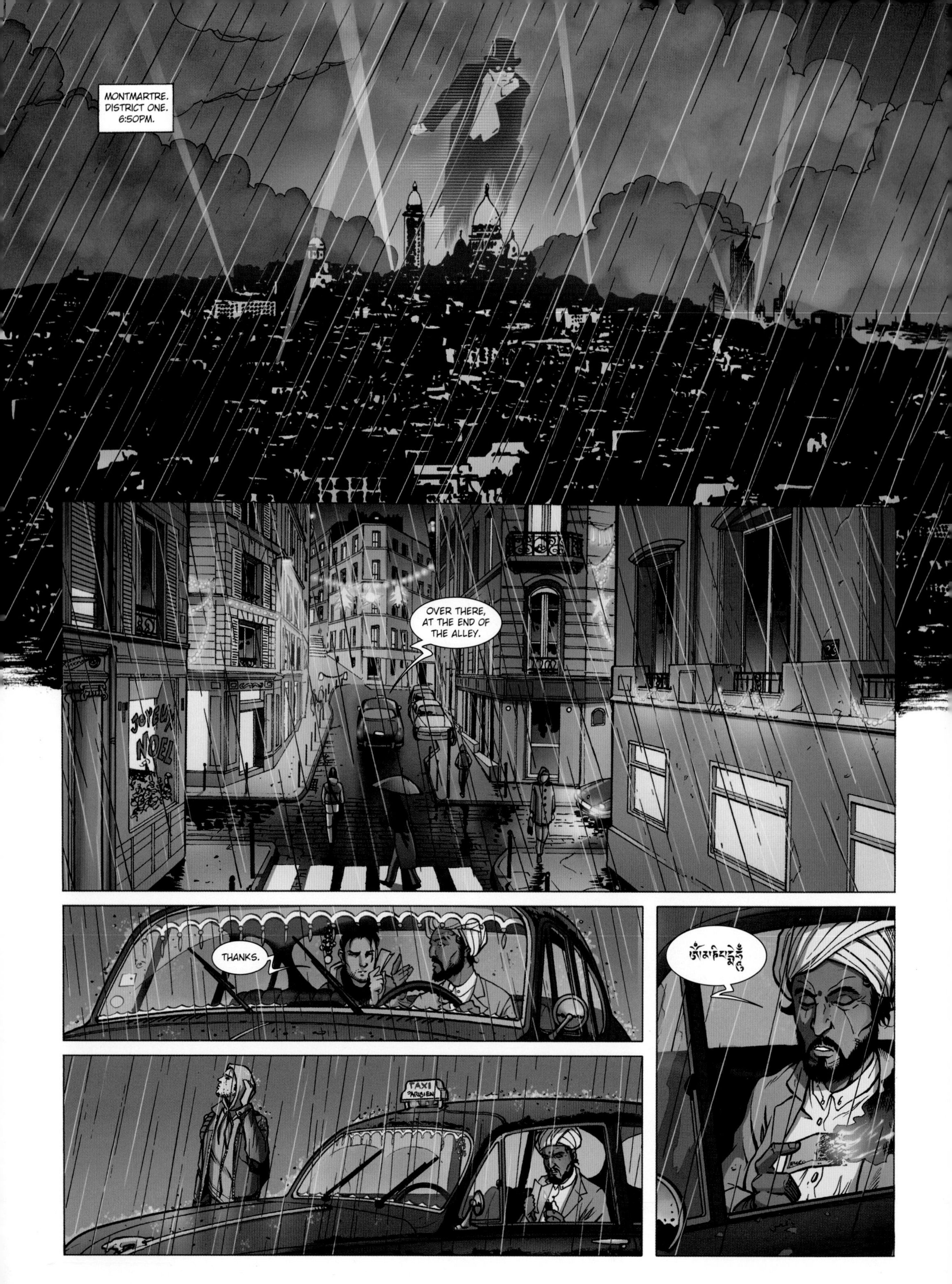
MONTMARTRE.
DISTRICT ONE.
6:50PM.
OVER THERE, AT THE END OF THE ALLEY.
"JOYEUX NOEL"
THANKS.
ཨོཾ་མ་ཎི་པདྨེ་ཧཱུྃ
TAXI PARISIEN

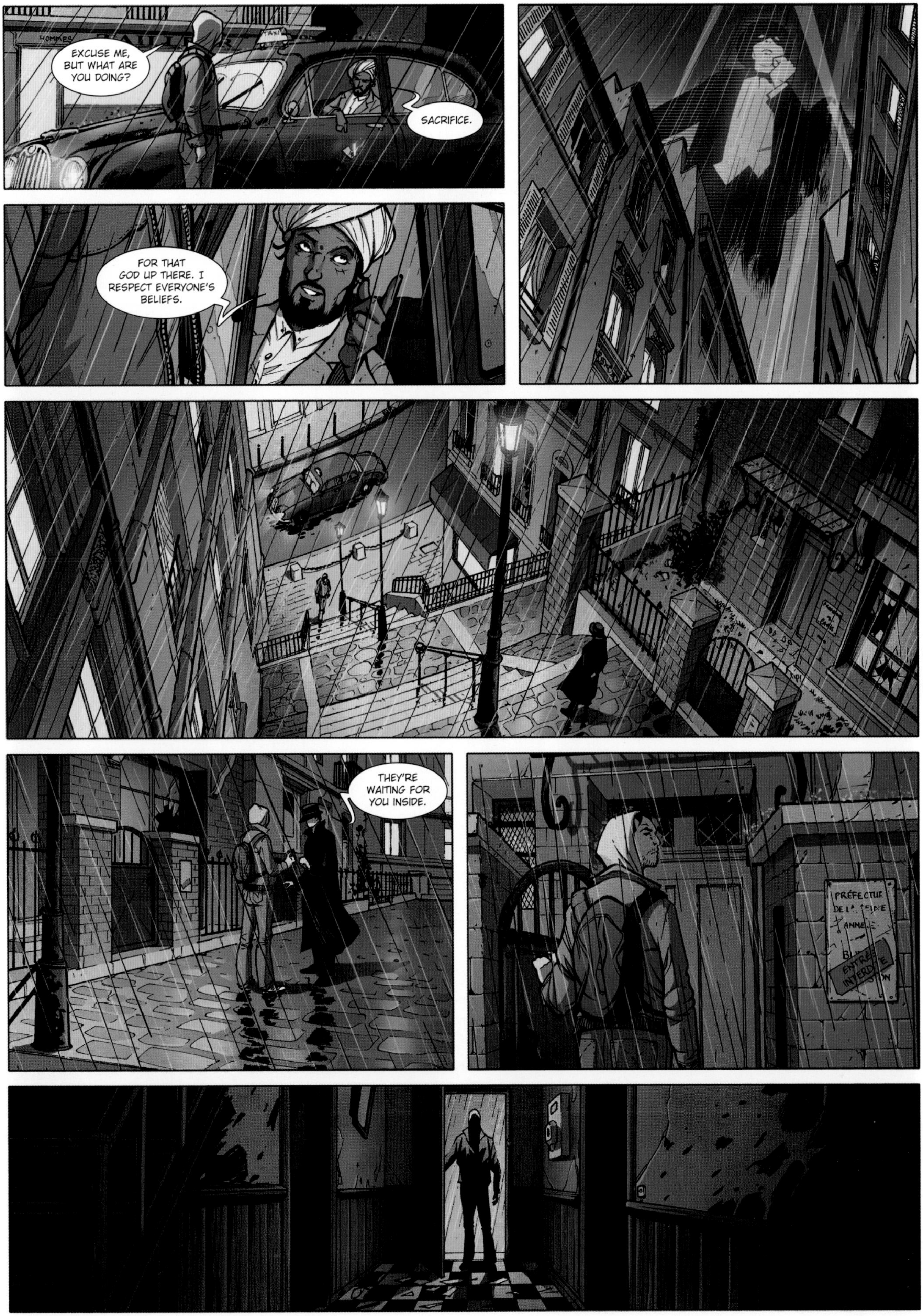
EXCUSE ME, BUT WHAT ARE YOU DOING?
SACRIFICE.
FOR THAT GOD UP THERE. I RESPECT EVERYONE'S BELIEFS.
THEY'RE WAITING FOR YOU INSIDE.

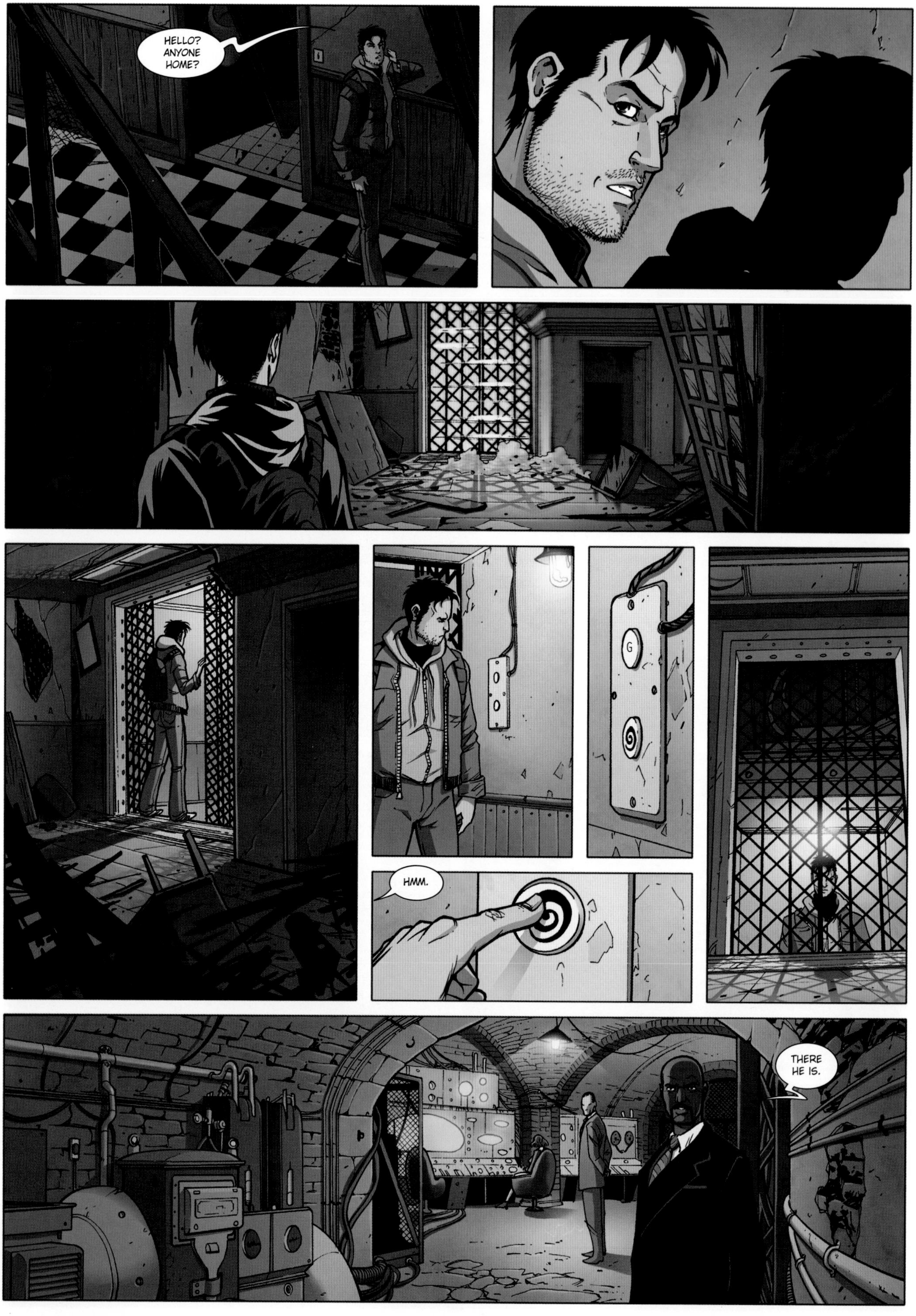
HELLO? ANYONE HOME?
HMM.
THERE HE IS.

HOLY SHIT...

WAIT... DON'T TELL ME.

I READ TONS OF STORIES ABOUT THIS PLACE WHEN I WAS A KID.

FANTÔM

WE'RE IN FANTOMA'S SECRET CAVE!

NOT JUST HIS.

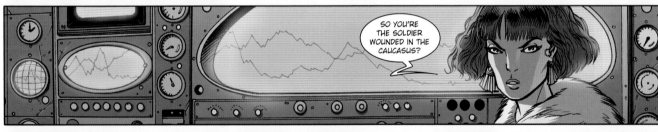

SO YOU'RE THE SOLDIER WOUNDED IN THE CAUCASUS?

SO HAPPY YOU CAME, BRAFFORT. THIS IS MY SCIENTIFIC ADVISOR AND FRIEND, CLEO VILLANOVA.

I'VE HEARD OF YOU...

I WROTE A POPULAR THESIS ON PSYCHOGEOGRAPHY.

THAT'S IT. MY SISTER HAS IT. I SAW IT THIS MORNING.

REMARKABLE COINCIDENCE.

JOEL, YOU KNOW I DON'T BELIEVE IN COINCIDENCE. TELL HIM.

MR. BRAFFORT, THIS IS MUCH MORE THAN A SUPERCRIMINAL'S CAVE. IT HAS TO DO WITH WHAT HAPPENED TO YOU THIS MORNING AT THE PREFECTURE.

YOU MEAN THE ANOMALIES?

WHAT DO YOU KNOW ABOUT THEM?

NOT MUCH. I JUST GOT BACK TO PARIS YESTERDAY.

STOP ME IF I'M WRONG, BUT... THEY'RE ASSEMBLAGES OF OBJECTS THAT MIMIC LIFE.

MORE OR LESS. THE PRESS COVERS THE MOST REMARKABLE CASES, LIKE THE GHOSTBOARDER, BUT THERE ARE HUNDREDS OF THEM. EVEN THE APS UNDERESTIMATES THEIR NUMBER.

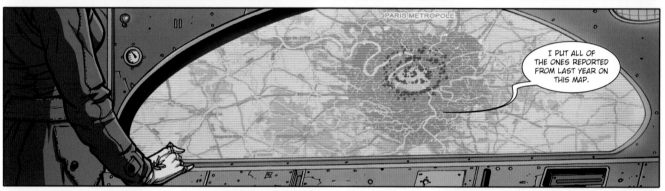

PARIS METROPOLE

I PUT ALL OF THE ONES REPORTED FROM LAST YEAR ON THIS MAP.

YOU SEEM TROUBLED.

I... IT'S NOTHING.

THE SPIRAL STARTS IN MONTMARTRE. FROM THIS BUILDING, I GUESS?

EXACTLY.

CLEO WAS TRYING TO LOCATE THE SOURCE, AND FINALLY FOUND IT HERE. SINCE IT'S AN ANNEX OF THE OLD SEINE PREFECTURE, I REQUESTED IT FOR STUDY.

THAT'S HOW WE FOUND THE ELEVATOR AND THIS CELLAR.

SO FANTOMA WAS A COP?

NO. HE VANISHED IN 1925. SOMEONE ELSE MOVED IN AFTER HIM AND STAYED 'TIL AT LEAST 1940.

SHOW HIM, ASSAN.

SINCE NO ONE KNOWS HIS NAME, WE CALL HIM "THE MASKED MAN."

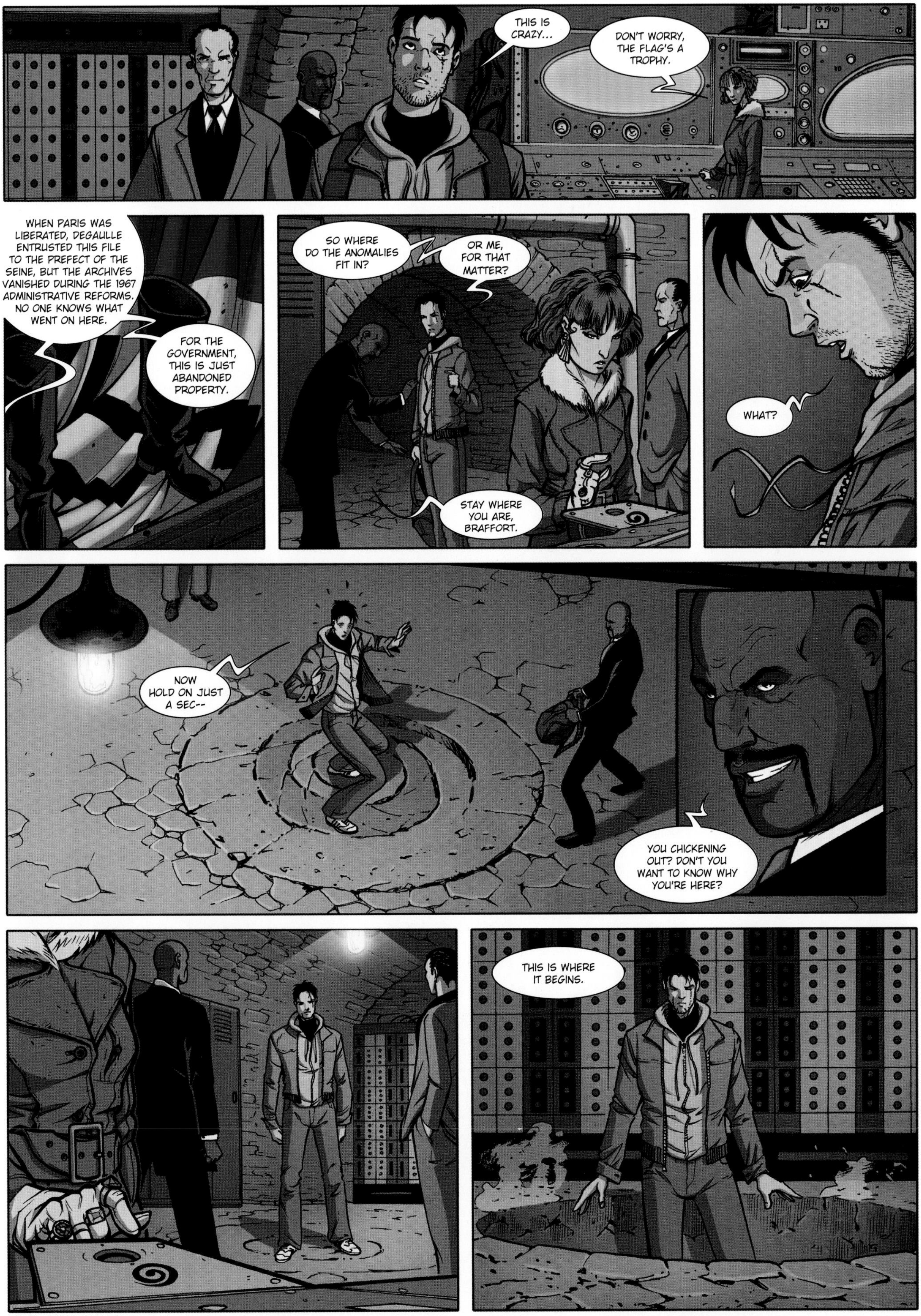
THIS IS CRAZY...
DON'T WORRY, THE FLAG'S A TROPHY.
WHEN PARIS WAS LIBERATED, DEGAULLE ENTRUSTED THIS FILE TO THE PREFECT OF THE SEINE, BUT THE ARCHIVES VANISHED DURING THE 1967 ADMINISTRATIVE REFORMS. NO ONE KNOWS WHAT WENT ON HERE.
FOR THE GOVERNMENT, THIS IS JUST ABANDONED PROPERTY.
SO WHERE DO THE ANOMALIES FIT IN?
OR ME, FOR THAT MATTER?
STAY WHERE YOU ARE, BRAFFORT.
WHAT?
NOW HOLD ON JUST A SEC--
YOU CHICKENING OUT? DON'T YOU WANT TO KNOW WHY YOU'RE HERE?
THIS IS WHERE IT BEGINS.

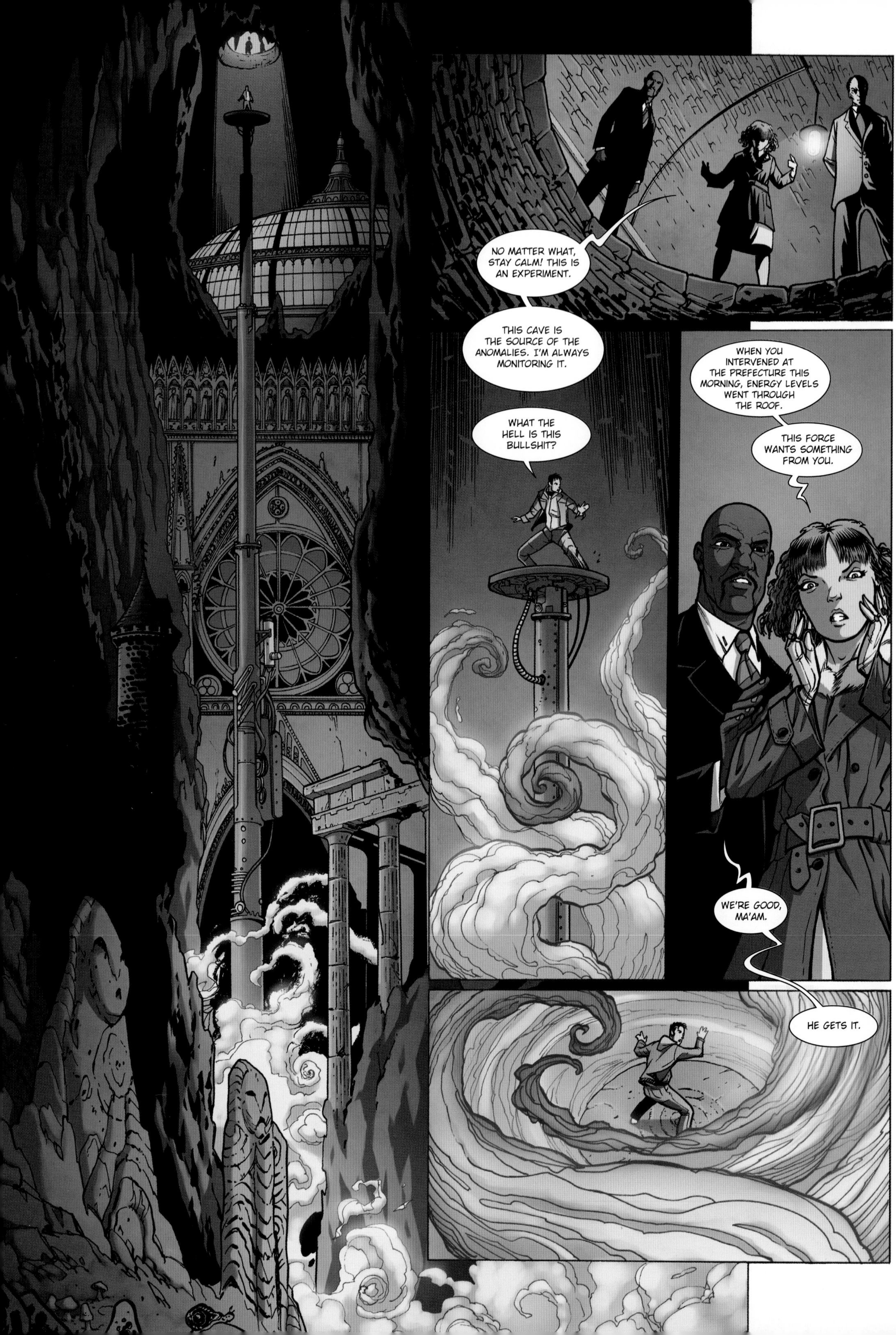
NO MATTER WHAT, STAY CALM! THIS IS AN EXPERIMENT.
THIS CAVE IS THE SOURCE OF THE ANOMALIES. I'M ALWAYS MONITORING IT.
WHAT THE HELL IS THIS BULLSHIT?
WHEN YOU INTERVENED AT THE PREFECTURE THIS MORNING, ENERGY LEVELS WENT THROUGH THE ROOF.
THIS FORCE WANTS SOMETHING FROM YOU.
WE'RE GOOD, MA'AM.
HE GETS IT.

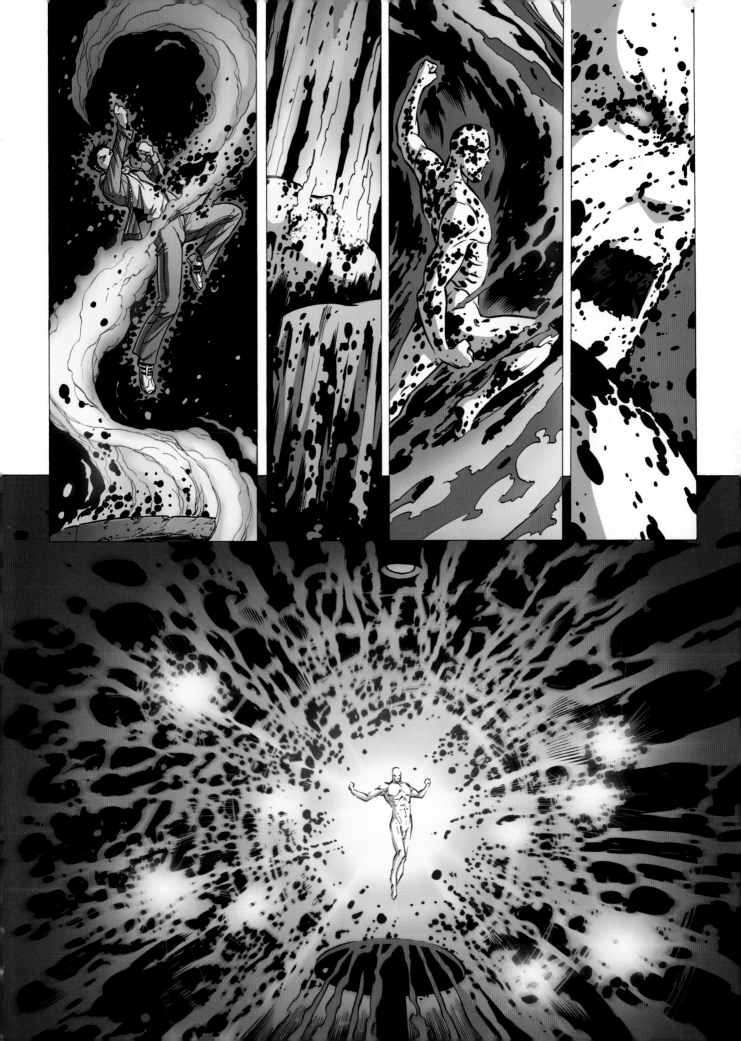

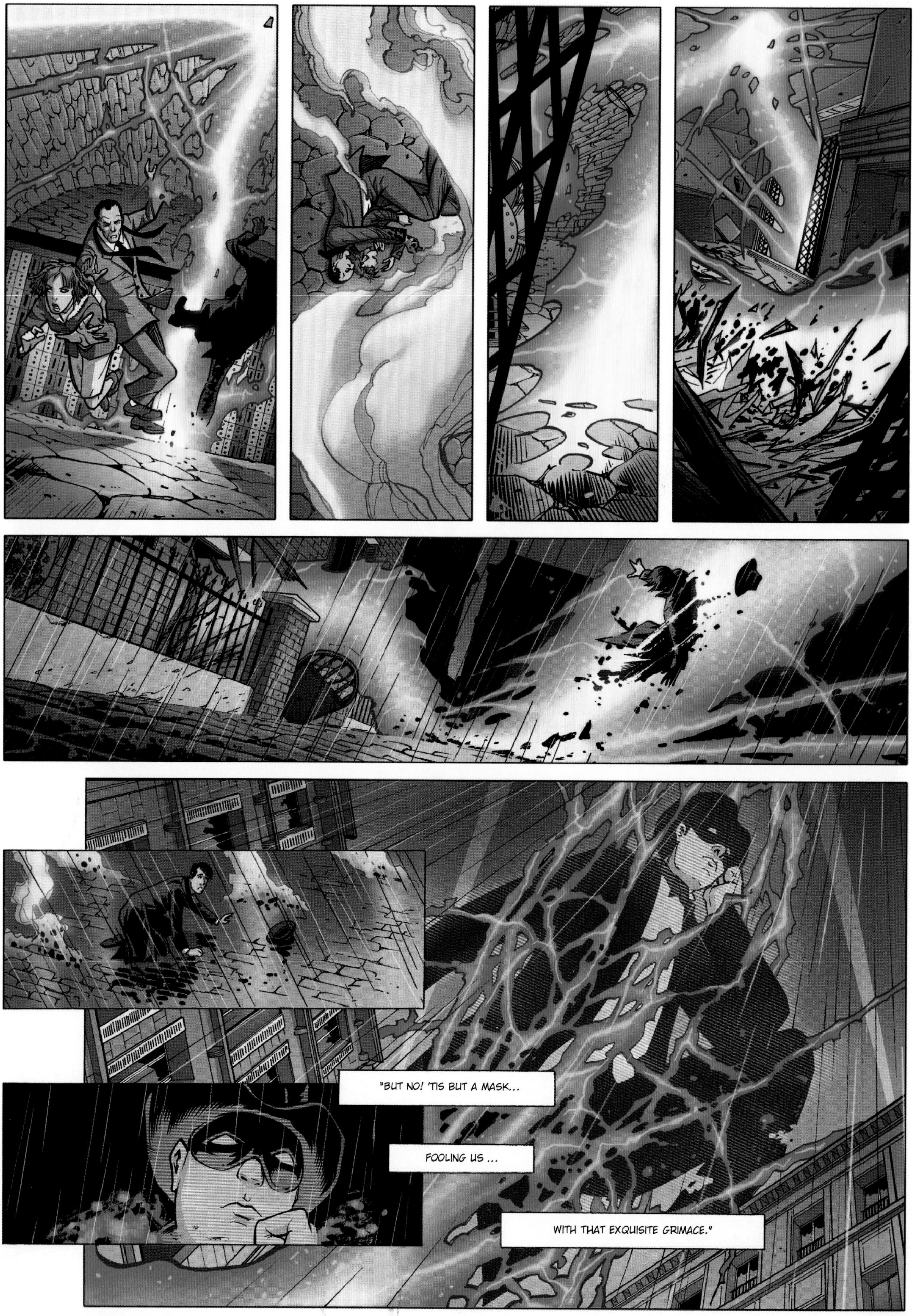
"BUT NO! 'TIS BUT A MASK...
FOOLING US ...
WITH THAT EXQUISITE GRIMACE."

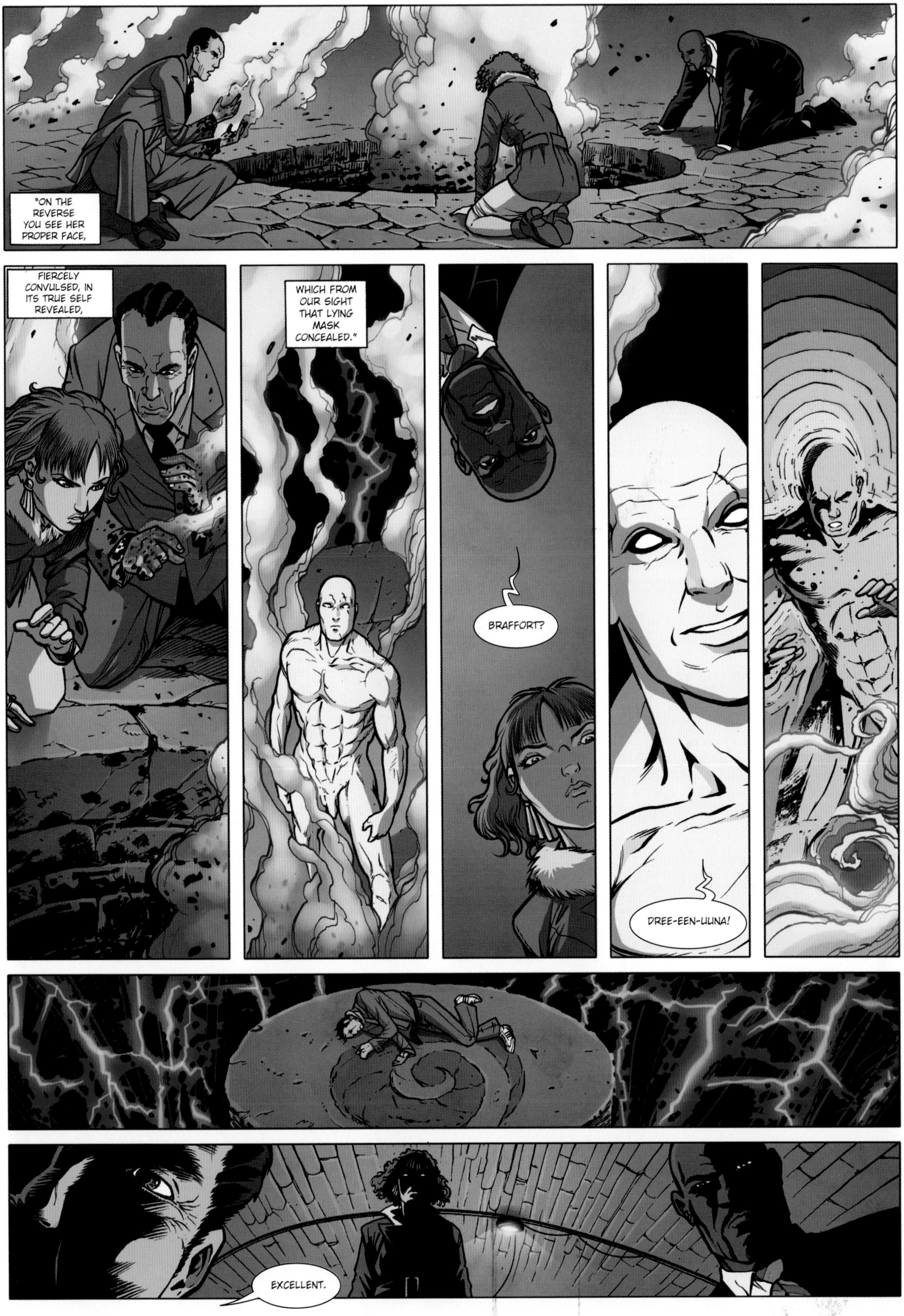
"ON THE REVERSE YOU SEE HER PROPER FACE,
FIERCELY CONVULSED, IN ITS TRUE SELF REVEALED,
WHICH FROM OUR SIGHT THAT LYING MASK CONCEALED."
BRAFFORT?
DREE-EEN-UUNA!
EXCELLENT.

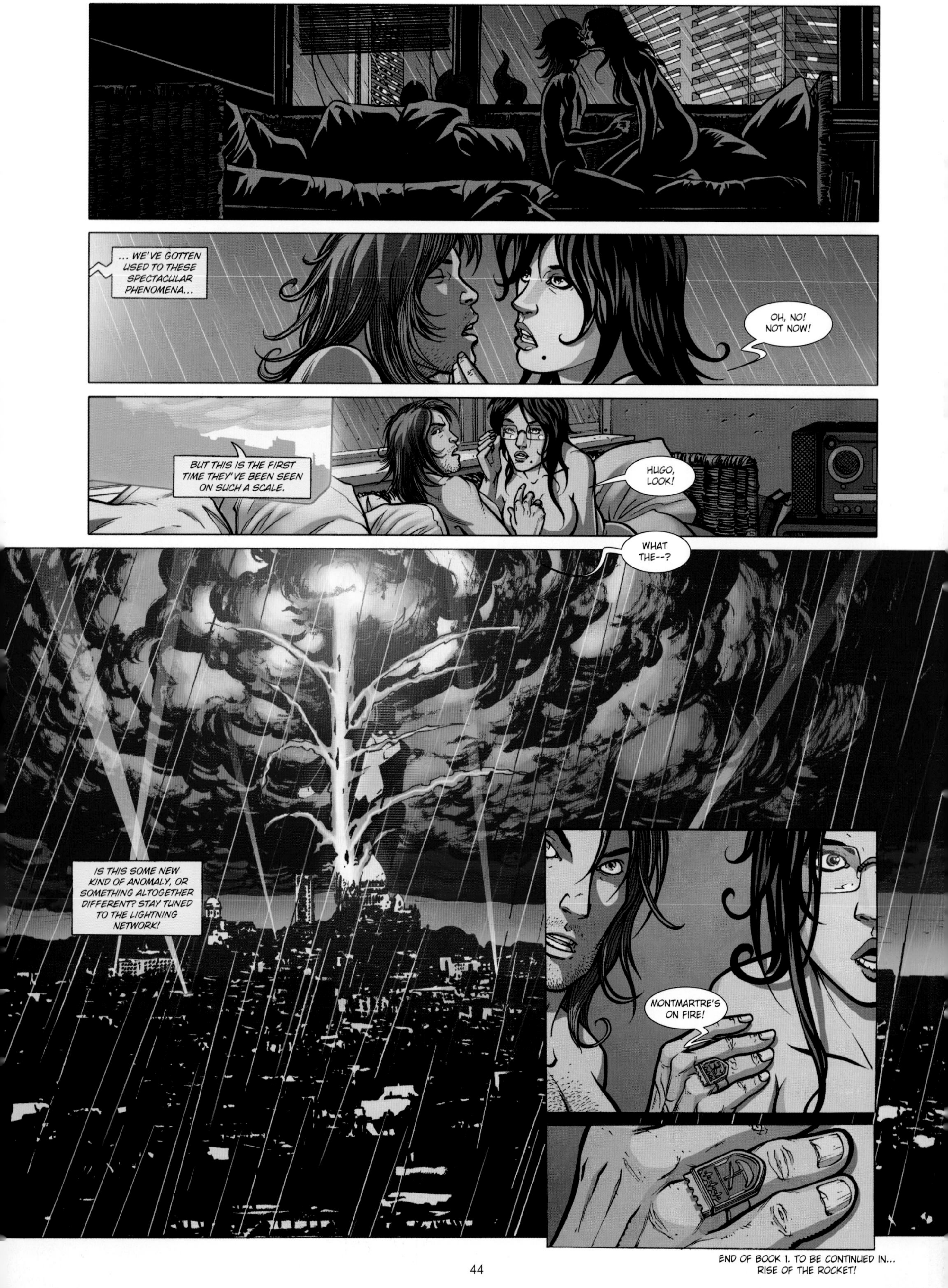
... WE'VE GOTTEN USED TO THESE SPECTACULAR PHENOMENA...
OH, NO! NOT NOW!
BUT THIS IS THE FIRST TIME THEY'VE BEEN SEEN ON SUCH A SCALE.
HUGO, LOOK!
WHAT THE--?
IS THIS SOME NEW KIND OF ANOMALY, OR SOMETHING ALTOGETHER DIFFERENT? STAY TUNED TO THE LIGHTNING NETWORK!
MONTMARTRE'S ON FIRE!

END OF BOOK 1. TO BE CONTINUED IN... RISE OF THE ROCKET!

METROLOGY

= ALL THINGS PARISIAN IN (IM)MODERATION =

Search... → ✉ ⚡ 🕶 👑

= RECENT POSTS =

→ What Guy Debord should have told us

→ Renovating Les Halles (again?)

→ The Derivative or the art of fake IDs

→ Privatizing La Plaine

→ Jean Nouvel is alive and well

→ Chronicles of Chic: from Chanel to Gaultier

→ Holograms of criminals: Why not Lupin?

→ Nuclear threat in Saclay

→ What if the Lightning Network was an Anomaly?

→ Older posts

A Night at the BPA

by Zoe Kader

It's almost midnight when I show up at Pont Morland, on the border between the 4th and 12th arrondissements of Paritropolis (District 1). It's cold, which isn't surprising for December 22, and I feel the brief sting of hail on my cheek; tomorrow's forecasted rain is here ahead of schedule. Lt. Brousse warned me on the phone: "When the going gets rough, we could get sent anywhere in the metropolis. Even Sénart or Montmorency, way out in the woods. Dress for it."

APS management has put Officer Brousse in charge of press relations. My intentions were to spend a night embedded in the Squad and report freely about it – not on TV, where I usually appeared, but in writing, on my blog – and when I explained that to Brousse, he started backpedaling: "Units have a private, human dimension – you don't talk about that." (Implication: if you want celebrities or superstars, better stick with the prefecture). But I persisted. I called him back. I put together my best pieces and sent them to him. I think that won him over, because he finally gave me the green light. In a nicer, warmer voice.

So this afternoon, I went down Rue de Rivoli to do some shopping. Not exactly the greatest idea two days before Christmas, but I managed to snag an Etro overcoat and decent-looking Mellow Yellow boots (my wardrobe needed a makeover, anyway). For such a classy neighborhood, the atmosphere was kind of tense. In one of the boutiques, a violent argument broke out between the shoppers and the salesladies; they had to call the police. And when I came back out again, two men almost came to blows over a taxi. "It's this city," the one who wound up on the sidewalk muttered. "This insane city. It's not like it used to be anymore. I don't understand what's going on these days."

He was talking to himself, mumbling, shaking his head and twisting the handle of his Longchamp bag, overflowing with presents. He looked lost. And, oddly enough, he was the one I was thinking about when Lt. Brousse came out of the shadows, crossed the bridge, and came to greet me. Maybe because he had the exact opposite expression on his face: he was calm, untroubled, confident.

"I recognize you," he said, smiling, "but I still have to check your papers."

I was freezing: the Etro overcoat wasn't a good idea. Brousse took his time. You could tell from the shape of his shoulders that under his jacket he was well-built. Around us, cars were shooting out of Boulevard Bourdon and turning toward Pont d'Austerlitz. Between the long, straight Arsenal quays, a few pleasureboats bobbed lightly on the icy water (I thought all the sailors in Paris had retreated to the new port at Gennevilliers, but no). An aerodyne from the Prefecture flew by overhead then turned and headed for the old forensic institute. The metro went by, deafening.

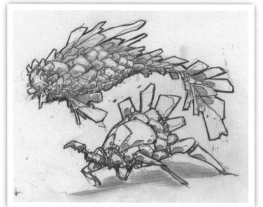

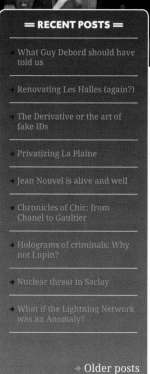

→ Next page

Brousse handed my papers back and led me down a flight of stone steps toward the water. "The APS maintains an operational HQ by City Hall," he explained, pushing open an iron gate half-hidden under the bridge. "But we can also scramble from here if need be, and I figured you might want to see our backup."

I followed him into an underground space that must have dated back to Louis XVIII. With its moss-covered, water-worn stone vaults and piles of fallen rock pushed to the corners, the place looked more like a natural cave than anything man-made. Fluorescent lighting from the ceiling gave off a pale light that wasn't doing anyone any favors: neither Brousse, whose face suddenly took on a greenish tint (I was glad I wasn't on camera), nor the three other APS agents who got up when we came in. Brousse introduced them: "Agent Lenclud. Agent Osman. Major Baronchelli."

I found out more about them as the night went on. Mohamed Osman had gone to law school and wanted to pick it up again, but his work with the Squad "ate up all his time." Hervé Baronchelli smoked like a chimney, didn't talk much, and liked being called "Baron." Twenty-five year-old Anne Lenclud was two months pregnant, but planned to take maternity leave "at the last possible second." I didn't know any of this when I shook her hand. All I knew was that she was giving my Mellow Yellow boots the stinkeye. She was in heavy-duty clodhoppers.

There was a thermos full of coffee on the table by the agents. Brousse poured me a cup, then led me into the depths of the hangar. The lower part of the curved walls disappeared behind a maze of shelves and metal lockers. Many of the anomalies the APS had seized over the last five years were piled in plastic bins, shapes both strange and familiar. Fragments sledgehammered from walls where Aramaic-looking geometric figures had appeared. Machines of all sizes (the biggest was about six feet and looked vaguely like a jackhammer with wings, but Brousse told me there were others even bigger in a District 3 warehouse). Machines! I've always found the word wanting. *Eppur si muove*, as Galileo said. *And yet it moves.*

And then there are the organisms.

Brousse pulls a drawer open and takes out something inert that looks like a crab, about a foot across, with six articulated legs made of nails, screws, and iron wire. He gives it a quick shake; the legs clink and clatter before falling motionless once more. If this horror was ever alive, it's dead now. But what kind of life-force ever animated it? That's the question.

"No one will ever know," Brousse said, as if reading my thoughts. "And you know why? Because of causal censorship."

Like most non-specialists, I know this expression. Sometimes I even use it myself (like here, on this blog, when I'm not talking about shopping). But I never really figured out what it meant. Brousse can tell. He gives me a half-grin. And the more he talks, the more the APS warehouse – with its vaulted stone ceilings and fluorescent lighting, its lockers stuffed with unidentified objects, and its taciturn agents – seems to herald a new world. This place is just the airlock.

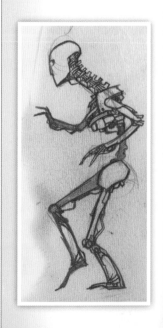

"It may seem hard to believe, but anomalies – even inert ones – are sensitive to changes in the human psyche. We can store them, classify them, catalog them, photograph or film them, but as soon as we try and analyze them in the lab, something comes up and throws a spanner in the works."

"What kind of something?"

"Coincidences. It's like the laws of probability get altered." Brousse looks at me and realizes he's lost me. With a sigh, he hands me the crab and asks me to hold it. I have to force myself. It's cold, pretty heavy, but – apparently – nothing more than an object. What's it got to do with probability?

"You work for a major TV network. You probably have science experts on call as consultants.

"OK, so close your eyes and picture one of them. Pretend you're giving him the anomaly and asking for a complete physiochemical rundown."

→ Next page

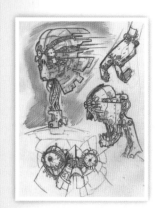

Two years ago, at La Defense, I covered a bomb scare. It was a homemade explosive device, and I interviewed a chemist from Saclay – Dr Gandji – about what it was made from. We'd gotten along. I can still see his round face, dark hair combed back. He wore a little diamond in one ear. I had no problem imagining him, crab in hand, in front of his electron microscope. (Actually, I'm sure he'd be delighted to study an anomaly. It's the dream of every scientist in Paritropolis).

"Alright," said Brousse. "Now try and get out of here."

He points to the door where we'd come in. "Try and keep in mind what you're up to: you're going to hand over the anomaly to an expert for analysis. Go on."

I look at the lieutenant, not really understanding what he wants from me. Lenclud, Osman, and the Baron are gathered behind their little table, waiting for my reaction. Walk out? For good? Give Gandji the crab?

This is a lot more than I ever hoped for from a night with the APS.

Without really meaning to, I start walking. But I've barely taken three steps when my foot snags on a cobblestone and I fall, face-first, flat on the wet floor.

"Careful," Brousse says without moving. "It gets dangerous from here on out."

"I just tripped," I tell him, getting back up. My Etro overcoat is ruined, but I couldn't care less. The crab's still in my hand, heavy, the story that could make my career. If the agents let me through, if I can really get out and call Gandji, I'll be the first reporter to ever get an authentic analysis of a phenomenon that's stirred up curiosity the world over. I start walking again. The door's only ten feet away when I feel something tickling my forehead. I look up. Just overhead, a stone from the vault looks like it's about to come loose. Maybe from the vibrations of the nearby metro? It's shivering almost imperceptibly and all around it, the more-than-hundred year-old mortar is crumbling, sifting down in a fine rain. I take another step. A chunk of plaster the size of a fist suddenly breaks free and smacks me in the shoulder. It doesn't hurt that much, but I still let out a yelp, then break into a run for the door. I grab the knob and turn. It comes off in my hand while the loose block of stone behind me crashes to the ground.

"Starting to get the idea?" Brousse asks, walking over.

I'm frozen in place, out of breath, the broken doorknob in one hand and the crab in the other. Brousse pats my shoulder gently and takes back the anomaly. I don't resist. The huge block of stone sits on the floor about three feet away. It must weigh about a hundred pounds. I look up at the gaping hole in the vaulted ceiling. It looks like someone yanked a tooth out of an old guy's mouth.

"If you'd gotten past the door, you would've lost your balance on the quay and fallen into the river," says Brousse. "Or, if not exactly that, then something like it. If you'd somehow managed to get up to Pont Morland and hail a taxi, you'd probably have gotten into an accident. You might've tried calling your scientist to tell him you were coming, but your phone would've stopped working. Catch my drift?"

Brousse gives the crab a shake. "It's like the universe is trying to prevent us from analyzing these things. A kind of cosmic sanction. Like how you can't go faster than the speed of light. As soon as you start trying, incredible things happen. The laws of causality are upended."

Cigarette dangling from his lips, the Baron ghosts past me and grabs the broken doorknob, heading for the door. I keep staring at the hole in the vault and at long last, I hear myself say in a samll voice, "But what force is causing this? What is it?"

Brousse shrugs and turns to put the crab back in its locker. "Probably the same one that created the anomalies in the first place, but that's just a theory. Without detailed study, that's all we can say. Some physicists call them large-scale quantum phenomena. Observer effect. Know what that means?"

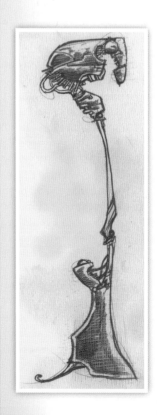

→ Next page

I shake my head. No. At the other end of the cavern, Brousse snorts. "Me neither, not really. But it's not important. You can live without knowing. And the Squad has its own theories, anyway."

I'm on more familiar terrain here. Commissioner Reines – the boss of the APS – has often expressed his conviction that the anomalies are linked to the actions of Prefect Beauregard, who's in charge of the city. In support of this theory, all Reines has are a handful of coincidental dates (the very first anomalies appeared shortly after the Prefect was appointed). But – as I just found out to my chagrin – coincidences are a fundamental part of this very deep mystery. Over the last five years, Beauregard has turned the city of Paris upside down. His influence on architecture, fashion, design, culture, and social habits has been enormous. His obsession with size and scale, and his taste for retro-futurism have changed the very soul of the capital.

Observer effect? Crossing to the table where Anne Lenclud and Mohamed Osman were having their umpteenth coffee, I cast about for the best way to put this idea into words. Was it possible that by changing Parisians' perception of their own city, by reinstating the cult of heights, of Golden Age icons like Fantoma, Beauregard had contributed to the emergence of... what, exactly? A new kind of urban physics? When you said it like that, it sounded absurd. But when you looked at it in the light of Cleo Villanova's role at the prefecture, all kinds of possibilities opened up. Urban physics. Psychogeography. It all seemed to come from the same occult logic, as irresistible as it was intangible.

In the end, maybe the man on Rue de Rivoli was right. I wanted to tell Brousse and the others about the incident. I wanted to ask them if it had been a kind of coincidence in advance. Did the city think through its inhabitants? No idea like that had ever crossed my mind before tonight. The air in the warehouse had unexpected speculative effects! But just as I was about to open my mouth, the lieutenant's cell phone went off. He picked up, listened, nodded twice, then turned toward his agents. "River police have spotted a mass moving toward Île Seguin. Let's go."

Somehow – I can't explain it – the Baron had managed to fix the door; thirty second later, we were outside. Three APS Zodiacs were waiting for us at the quay. Brousse dragged me into the first one and before I could turn around to see if Lenclud, Osman, and the Baron were behind us, the Zodiac had passed Pont Morland's old lock, made a hairpin turn, and headed west, kicking up a plume of spray. I felt like I was taking a shower with all my clothes on (goodbye for good to my new overcoat). I sneaked a peek at Brousse. The lights of the Arab World Institute lit up his face intermittently, before giving way swiftly to the shadows of Pont de Sully. We skirted Île St.-Louis on the right. Brousse's face was totally dry, but that wasn't why he was smiling. It was because everything that was happening – night shift at the warehouse, the river police call, the Zodiac's speed and the roar of its engines – he loved. I didn't need to see his face, or hear him say a word. It was as though I could hear his thoughts – I'm in the Anomalous Phenomena Squad. I fight to loosen Prefect Beauregard's hold on Paris. I neutralize unidentified entities that threaten the safety of the citizens. I fly down the river, through the night, toward unknown danger.

What could be better?

It took us twenty minutes to reach Boulogne and see the shores of Seguin Island. The moving mass the river police had reported reacted to our arrival. It turned weightily toward us and, in doing so, smacked one of the piers of the Pont de Sèvres with a dull boom, like a container ship.

"Good God," Brousse said, gripping my shoulder. "Look at that, Zoe. It's gigantic!"

What happened next is all over the news...

■